First published in 2003

Allen & Unwin
83 Alexander Street
Crows Nest NSW 2065
Australia
Phone: (61 2) 8425 0100
Fax: (61 2) 9906 2218
Email: info@allenandunwin.com
Web: www.allenandunwin.com

National Library of Australia
Cataloguing-in-Publication entry:
Paul, Anthea.
          Girlosophy: the breakup survival kit.

          ISBN 1 74114 077 3.
          1.Interpersonal relations. 2. Love. 3. Separation (Psychology).
          4. Women – Psychology. 5. Young women – Life skills guides. I. Title.

158.1

Concept by Anthea Paul
Art Direction and Design by Justine O'Donnell for jmedia design, Sydney, Australia
Additional Art Direction by Anthea Paul
Photography by Anthea Paul
Additional photography by Ashley de Prazer (pp 37, 40, 118, 133, 141, 163), Chris Jones
(pp 52, 61, 84), Lawrence Dowd (pp 66, 100, 122, 142) and Marcus Clinton (p 64)
Illustrations by Justine O'Donnell, Anthea Paul and Sally Prisk
Printed in China by Imago

10 9 8 7 6 5 4 3 2 1

ophy

THE BREAKUP SURVIVAL KIT

anthea paul

ALLEN&UNWIN

'THERE'S AN ART TO WIPING OUT'.
Kelly Slater, 6-time world champion surfer

For my sister, Kate and for Joey Quinn
with love and thanks

Contents

SPIRIT

journal

meditation

chakras

Introduction

Welcome to *girlosophy* — *The Breakup Survival Kit*! This book is for anyone who's ever been in a relationship, ended one, had one ended on them or who wants to end one. Relationships are key experiences in life and play a huge role in our personal development. They are one of the main reasons we are here on earth, for we are here to love and our connections with others give us this opportunity. The defining moments in our lives are those which result from or happen through our relationships, for better or worse.

Relationships — everyone is fascinated by them, they are what we endlessly talk about and analyze, figuring out strategies to improve or end them, pondering their idiosyncrasies and often just plain obsessing about them. Let's face it, relationships are where it's at! Fun, frustrating, frivolous, frenetic, fantastic … when they are good, relationships give us a sense of being part of something larger and often a sense of identity, not to mention the security and joy of loving and of being loved. But no matter what the reasons the end of any important relationship hits hard. Our security zone is suddenly on red-alert and our mind, body and spirit feel threatened. When a relationship we have come to rely on breaks up, we may feel as though we're under siege. One of the purposes of this book is to examine what it's really all about — which is change! It's actually about change and how you adapt to it and then, in the process of adapting, how you flow with the outcome. For relationships are nothing, if not life-changing. Good or bad, long or short, relationships force you to grow. We are never the same after a relationship as we were at its beginning. And much of the time, that is a good thing.

The Breakup Survival Kit celebrates the uniqueness and beauty of our individual relationships and explores how we can retain a sense of self in the process of relationship changes and their aftermath.

Why *The Breakup Survival Kit*?

Because life is all about love! Or love gone awry or wrong — horribly or otherwise — or love somehow lost. Love is still the biggest show in town and everyone has a part to play … sometimes due to circumstances beyond our control — and let's face it, in the bigger scheme of things circumstances are always beyond our control — things just don't pan out the way we intended. Blame it on the planets or the Year of the Goat or Rat or whatever it happens to be, but sometimes the Universe just hands you a whopper. You break up with or separate from the one person you thought would be in your life forever. He or she is moving out and moving on. Or maybe you are. Maybe you don't know what you have (or had) or where you two are at the moment. It could be a temporary break that turns permanent or it could be a much-needed rest for each of you to get your bearings before you reconvene at a later date. Maybe you left clutching your laptop, your pot plants and a few fridge magnets, and have no idea where you'll end up. Maybe there was a final note left in your locker at school. Perhaps a third party is involved and the torments of your newly fired-up imagination get worse daily. And to top that, your inbox is no longer filled with sweet nothings. Even worse (and yes, things can always be worse!) perhaps the third party is someone you trust or know well and you now have to contend with your best friend and the one-time love of your life getting together. Two exes at one fell swoop! Maybe you have to see your ex every day at school or college or work. Perhaps you feel your friends have abandoned you now that you've broken up with your partner. Whatever the details, you now find yourself in relationship hell or, at the very least, relationship limbo. It doesn't look good from where you are sitting but you know you're going to have to get through it — although how you will remains to be seen. One thing is for sure: you're in dire need of some coping strategies.

However, it's not all bad news! The good news is that even if you think your current love life is a disaster or simply non-existent, you're in for a (nice) surprise. Take heart, because you're in transition and that's a very powerful place to be. Anytime you go through change that is profound (i.e. it's noticeable and absolutely can't be ignored), it's a real chance for growth. This is when you get a glimpse of your own soul — of who you really are — and so it's actually a great opportunity to focus on what you really want for your life and become more comfortable with what's right for you, now. In my experience, often the nicest, most compassionate people you come across are those who have suffered the odd setback or perhaps even real tragedy, they have lived through that much quoted 'dark night of the soul' everyone must experience for spiritual growth. In fact, there is a good case to support the view that people who have not experienced some sort of pain, disappointment or heartache in life are the ones to be careful of, for they can inflict real pain on others without — and this is the kicker — even being aware of it. They simply don't grasp it, because it just doesn't register with them. The truth is that not being able to imagine what intense pain feels like means it's a lot easier to unwittingly inflict it.

But the focus of these pages is actually YOU, not THEM — which is one of the first things we have to get straight.

What awaits you within these pages is more than just advice on how to 'get over it' or 'get on with it', although these issues are certainly central — you will learn ways to push through the immediate pain to emerge stronger, wiser and more confident. It's not about avoidance, it's all about facing up and then facing off, if and when necessary! True to girlosophy form there is no such thing as failure, there's only progress. And we'll focus on that.

A break in the continuity of any relationship can cause stress and distress and require a recovery period with some heavy-duty reorientation — that is the reason for *The Breakup Survival Kit*. It's for you.

What kinds of relationships are covered in *The Breakup Survival Kit*?

The relationships covered in *The Breakup Survival Kit* are not restricted to the standard romantic mixed-gender relationship although this will probably be the relationship that is the most applicable to you. I use the terms he/she/they interchangeably and as loosely as possible, leaving the specifics up to you.

The principles I discuss are virtually the same for every relationship although the degree of intensity and the longevity of the relationship in question will obviously play a huge role in determining the level of trauma or pain experienced. The material within these pages can be applied to the following relationships:

* A relationship which is platonic (friendship-based). This can be between people of the same or different gender (based on emotional content only);
* A relationship that is heterosexual–romantic (mixed gender with emotional content and a physical/sexual component);
* A relationship that is homosexual–romantic (same gender with emotional content and a physical/sexual component);
* A relationship that is based on blood relations or has a family context.

Phew! The point is, there are so many variations on what constitutes a relationship. If you think you have one, then as far as this book is concerned, you do. I have tried to keep the references and descriptions as gender-neutral as possible to cover as many situations and combinations as there are readers and specifics. Please adapt and apply these where relevant and/or necessary at your own discretion. It's free-form, for your maximum application.

I also note that, contrary to what is generally assumed, guys suffer just as much as girls at the end of a significant relationship. Sometimes more because they often don't have as many outlets as girls and most women do talk about what they're going through. So I hope the book can be of help to guys too. Do the world (or the next person in their life) a huge favor: pass it on to your brothers and male friends. Guys need our support at these times too, they are just less likely to be showing what they're going through. Be on the lookout for signs of their suffering so you can help them too.

In addition, I also recognize that certain relationships end due to the death of one of the partners and it is my sincere hope that some of the material in this book will benefit anyone enduring the grief associated with this most extreme form of relationship termination. I have visited websites related to this and had numerous emails from people who have experienced the death of their life partner and been devastated at finding themselves alone and without their primary relationship, unexpectedly or otherwise. Those brave souls who somehow manage to get on with their lives with courage in the face of incredible stress and suffering can inspire us all, for they know the pain of the ultimate relationship breakup, a breakup for which there can be absolutely no negotiation.

What could possibly help me now?

Don't worry, this is where you'll find the goods! As you'll discover, *The Breakup Survival Kit* is your personal mind–body–spirit guide to constructively using everything that life gives you relationship-wise. It's about finding the positive seeds of the future in the messy wash-up of entanglement! The thing is, whether you perceive them as good or bad, all relationships are gifts from the Universe and they are designed so you can keep on becoming ... yourself. In this book you'll not only find the relief you've been seeking, you'll also have a lot of questions answered and find a few home truths. Not only will you truly be able to 'get over it', but you will do so with increased self-knowledge — and with your dignity intact.

If you can get your head around this, soon you'll be exploring new dimensions of yourself and others (maybe even your ex) will be open-mouthed in their admiration. You are about to experience the glory of being a Phoenix rising! As a result you may find others come to you for advice the next time they go through a relationship crisis. And at that point you will understand the true meaning of compassion and empathy, which are the keys to your new life. When this happens, you'll understand that you've truly come a long way, baby...

What's in it for me?

Well may you ask! In true girlosophy-style, this book covers the chakras so you can work out where you need to do some spiritual, emotional and/or physical healing work. Also included are mantras, affirmations and meditations to incorporate into your new daily routine for your new Self ... well, you needed a new one didn't you? It's time to get out of that rut. It has been said that 'pain is simply weakness leaving the body', so if there's going to be pain, you may as well make it work for you. If you transmute your pain it can make you stronger and become an effective tool for personal gain.

This time can potentially be the most devastating time of your life or the most constructive, depending on your attitude. I say potentially, because your free will dictates how you act and react, the moods you experience and the decisions you make. There are no absolutes — it's up to you and the specifics of your situation. And there is no time to waste, because you have your destiny to get on with — the grieving process must be honored, but it's only one part of the whole picture. Life must go on and so must you!

Will I ever feel 'normal' again?
Definitely — that's if you were normal to begin with! The purpose of *The Breakup Survival Kit* is to help you figure out as soon as possible how to change mental, emotional and physical gears so you can get back on your personal mission as smoothly and as quickly as possible. The book also covers some of the warning signs, including things to watch out for next time (and you can bet you'll wish you'd had this stuff earlier) — I call them 'red flags'. Soon, you'll be in the fast lane once more and misery will no longer be your companion! girlosophy is all about helping you with the quickest recovery possible so you can move up to another level of life mastery.

The crying game ... why does this feel like it will never end?
Unsure if you're breaking up or breaking down? If you're right in a breakup now, the chances are you feel like you're doing both. No doubt you've shed a lake full of tears already and although I can't be there to pass the tissues, I am passing on something that I think you'll find a whole lot more useful: a guide to sustain you while you're going through it. This is a stressful time and you may be extremely fragile, so you need the support of friends and family and maybe even a counselor. There is an important section on depression, how to recognize the symptoms of depression in others and in yourself, and what to do about depression if you think you are suffering from it or if a temporary depression becomes chronic or long-term.

Whether the relationship you've been in lasted three weeks, three years or even longer, I hope you've had someone there to hold your hand and make you endless cups of tea! And you can take (some sort of) comfort in this fact: we've all been there. While it's certainly not pleasant and it's pretty much agony when you're in it, know this: you will get over it. You may or may not reunite with your ex, or even see or speak to them again, but at the very least I can assure you that within a short time you'll be a very different person from the one who has just picked up this book.

You'll find out how to switch your focus to the positive in any relationship break, so that you gain a new understanding. What is a break anyhow? It's down time and a point of separation. It's the often much-needed fork on the road in your journey which offers you a new path. And as it's always been your journey, you can choose to regard your ex as a traveling companion who came along for part of the ride. And now you're flying solo again … until the next time!

These are life-defining moments. If you heed the signs and get just a little distance and perspective on things, you'll see that no matter how bad they look at the time, the reality is that they're not all that bad. If you look at the upside until it becomes a habit then you won't even be able to relate to the down side. Soon, you'll be standing up straight, looking the world in the eye … and you'll keep on standing. In time, you may even see both the relationship and the breakup for what they truly were — which is the purpose of *The Breakup Survival Kit*: to get you to that point.

Are there any practical things I can do to speed things up?

Definitely. Getting a new routine is one of the fastest routes to recovery. To help you stay on track, at the end of the book you will find the 30-DAY BREAKUP RECOVERY JOURNAL, which is to encourage you to keep a written record of your progress. If you feel that you need to, you can extend it to 60 or 90 days or for as long as it takes. And hopefully the techniques and tips you incorporate into your daily routine will stay with you whatever your relationship status in the future.

What's love got to do with it?

As always, plenty. You can't mess with love and you certainly can't mess with karma! Whatever love you have created and shared is recorded in the Cosmos, which means that at the highest level you have succeeded, even if right now it looks (and feels) for all intents and purposes as if one or both of you have failed. I find it helpful to keep in mind at all times that there is a larger force at work than us. The larger force — love — holds that we are all in relationship to each other eternally, so in the higher scheme of things, you can never truly be separated or break up with anyone! You can just work off, balance or create karma through your various relationships. Each soul has its own mission designed by the Universe. If you can accept that then you're really advancing.

Above all, remember that you are unique, know that you are beautiful, special and totally lovable regardless of what goes down in your life. Your soul life is the important thing. Remember that it's all just a test.

One important thing I'd like to bring to your attention: LOVE is assumed throughout this book. If I sound clinical at times just remember: I'm trying to get you off the love drug. To function at all you have to be a bit objective, so occasionally I downplay the mushy stuff, while being absolutely certain that you and your ex were in love. But let's put that aside so we can deal with getting you up and at 'em again. And with that off my mind, let's get into yours!

A wise person once said that all actions are a movement towards or away from order. I hope you find *girlosophy — The Breakup Survival Kit* a helpful and constant companion for those times when you find yourself in the relationship wilderness. Above all, try to be happy now, look sharp and get ready because you never know what (or who) is coming...

And remember ... it's ALL good.

Anthea Paul

This chapter is about the Body. Your Body. We'll start with the body to make way for the mind to play catch up. It's the logical place to begin. The show — your show — must go on.

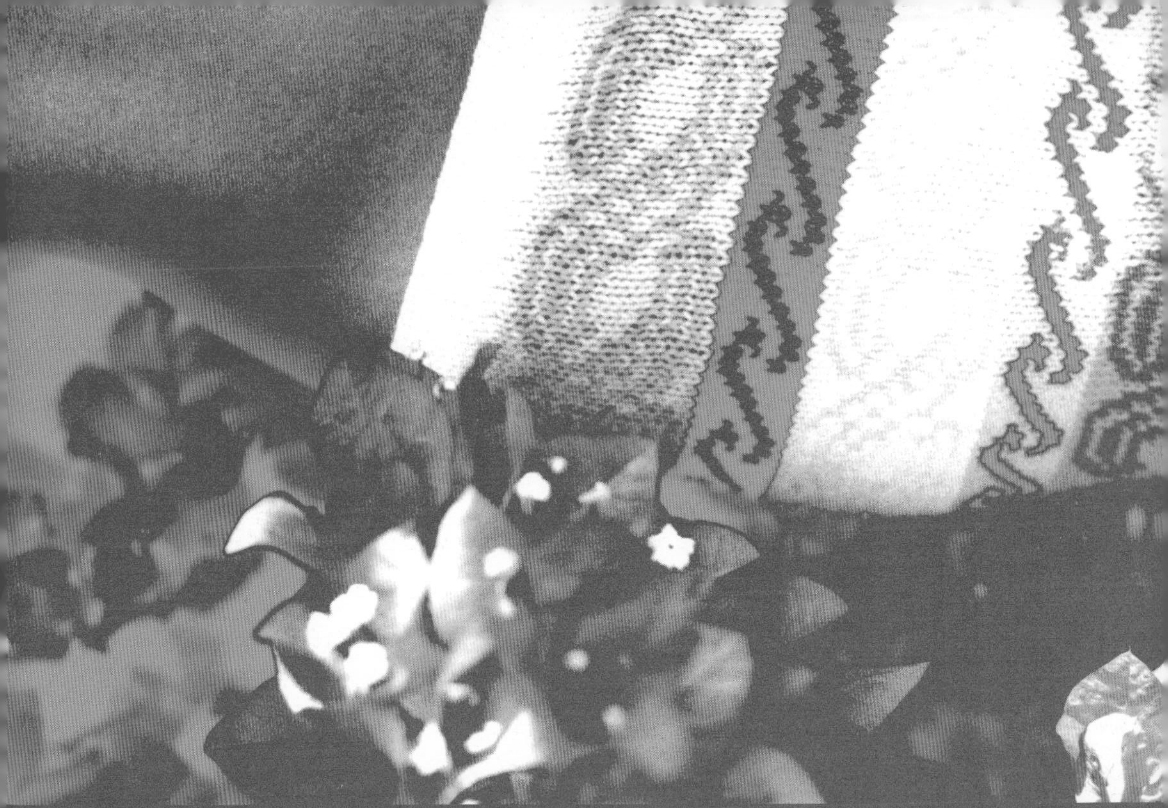

it's cleanup time

YOUR PHYSICAL SELF AND YOUR PHYSICAL SPACE

This is the section where you get out of your head and into your body ... phew! You knew it had to happen — no more chocolate biscuits or junk food while you grow roots on the couch. This is not the time to huddle with your doona pulled up to your chin watching the television or playing with your mobile phone, waiting for text messages. Out with the tissues and the tears. It's a whole new day and a whole new life. And whether you feel like it or not, you're going to be helped into it!

One thing to keep in mind as you read this section

YOU ARE NOT THE SAME BODY YOU WERE LAST WEEK OR EVEN YESTERDAY. YOU ARE CHANGING — ALL DAY EVERY DAY. THAT'S WHY THERE'S A NEW YOU ON A DAILY BASIS...

IT'S YOUR NEW LIFE

Your body is a chemistry experiment that is constantly in flux, and while you are going through 'stuff' — particularly as you do when you go through a breakup — you create a lot more toxins or free radicals than you do at other, more normal times. Breakups cause you to be stressed and depressed. Stress and depression create toxins in your body's system. Stress can also be the reason you're not sleeping well, you're feeling constantly exhausted even with enough sleep or getting ill — or just feeling less than your normal bouncy self. Both stress and depression, often interrelated, are health issues and are not to be taken lightly. They cause your chemistry to go a bit haywire, so in this section we'll look at ways to get you back on track health-wise.

IF YOU ARE SUFFERING
UNUSUAL OR PROLONGED
FEELINGS OF DEPRESSION AND
HAVE CONTEMPLATED DOING HARM
TO EITHER YOURSELF OR OTHERS,
YOU NEED TO GET PROFESSIONAL
SUPPORT AND HELP AT THIS TIME.
COUNSELING AND THERAPY CAN
BE TREMENDOUSLY EMPOWERING.
AS CAN MEDICAL ASSISTANCE.
DON'T BE AFRAID! IT'S OK TO ASK
FOR HELP. THERE ARE EXPERTS
WHO CAN HELP YOU. LIKEWISE, IF
SOMEONE YOU KNOW JUST ISN'T
GETTING OVER THE BREAKUP OF
THEIR RELATIONSHIP, AND YOU
THINK THEY MAY BE AT RISK, THEN
TAKE CHARGE OF THE SITUATION.
TALK TO THEM AND ASSIST THEM IN
GETTING THE MEDICAL ADVICE AND
PROFESSIONAL HELP THEY NEED.
YOU'LL BE A TRUE FRIEND INDEED!

27

Back to you on the couch.

The mere thought of leaving the house may sound like a really bad idea, but it's actually going to be a relief. And you'll have to trust me on this! Because when your muscles are aching from being pleasantly worked and when you're exhausted from too much fresh-air activity and you've had a gorgeous healthy meal, you're going to be sleeping better, thinking less about everything, feeling better and — here's the hidden bonus — looking better too.

DON'T WAIT! YOU WILL FEEL BETTER SOONER IF YOU... DO IT NOW.

In addition to getting into your physical body, in this section you're also going to get into your physical environment — the one that surrounds you at home or away! If you are living in a group environment (say with your family or in share-accommodation), you can still charge up and maximize the energies in your living space. If you live by yourself or if you have your own personal space, there are a number of things you can do to help put the past, including your ex, behind you. Energy clearing is personal work and it begins at home. In fact, before you leave the house, let's clean it up!

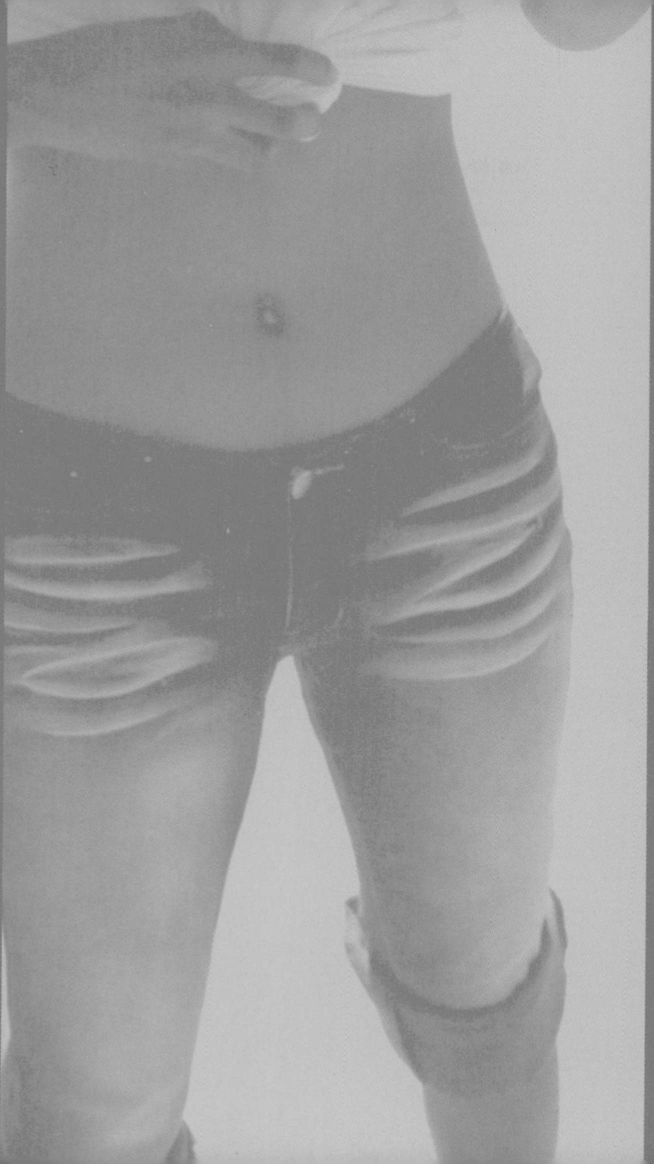

CLUTTER.
Clear it. Clean it. Recycle it. Get it OUT.

clear headspace

+

clear homespace

=

heart's peace

So while you've been mooning around the place, preoccupied with your ex, your living environment may have been lacking attention. Hmmmm. Paperwork piling up, cupboards a mess, bathroom not so sweet? Part of the Grand Fix-it Plan is to don gloves, plug in the vacuum cleaner and wield that feather duster: it's time to clean out the negative energy and get a new vibe going. Out with the old and in with the new. It's time to get the energy moving and you grooving again.

This chapter is about getting a clear physical view of things, which is crucial to your recovery. Sometimes this can give you the mental clarity you were seeking (more about this in the next chapter). When your eye travels unhindered over neat stacks of books on a bookshelf, shiny surfaces, fresh flowers in a vase and a neat bed, everything seems a bit more manageable. And when you're a girl on the go (which of course you are normally), who's got time to muddle through a muddle? Efficiency is easy when you commit to making a clean sweep. Once you get into it, you'll find boxing up and labeling can be a joy, and sorting and throwing out junk can be better (and more satisfying) than a hot date! Surveying the results of your sweat and tears will leave you feeling like Rocky at the top of the steps — or at least like Elle Woods on the graduation podium. And that's a promise.

FIRST THINGS FIRST. Put everything that reminds you of Him or Her away. Out of your line of vision means you can't trip into memory lane. And that is a good thing. If you get back together in the future, then you can drag it all out again. Or hopefully there will be new mementos for the 'new' relationship. Love letters, photographs, gifts, clothing, music, can all be reminders of what used to be. They can keep you reliving the past, and that's not where your future lies.

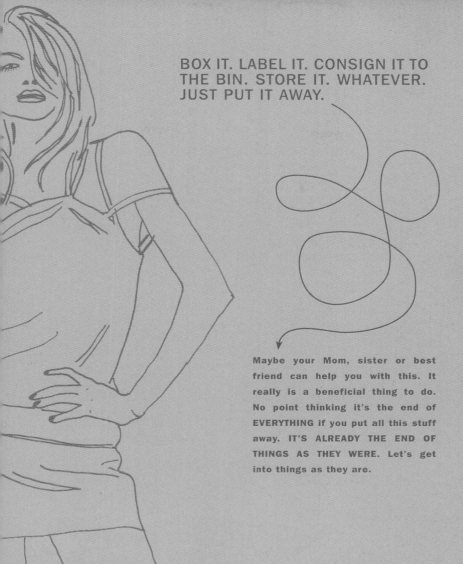

BOX IT. LABEL IT. CONSIGN IT TO THE BIN. STORE IT. WHATEVER. JUST PUT IT AWAY.

Maybe your Mom, sister or best friend can help you with this. It really is a beneficial thing to do. No point thinking it's the end of EVERYTHING if you put all this stuff away. IT'S ALREADY THE END OF THINGS AS THEY WERE. Let's get into things as they are.

Remember:

reality loves
a brave soul.
Right here.
Right now.

ROOM ... TO MOVE?

Maybe you need to create a new space for this new phase. When you intentionally create the space for the new, you let the Universe know you are ready to welcome it in. This can take many forms: an actual move into another room of the house you live in, an entirely new place to live, or just renovating the room you're already in. Change the color scheme. Pink is great for bringing in love and reducing tension. Green is soothing and gives a wonderful healing boost to your heart chakra (see Taking your chakras for a spin in the SPIRIT chapter) which is on overload during a breakup. A new room is a great cure-all. It gets you busy and focused. All of a sudden, you're on a mission! Get into the world of painting and scraping, window treatments, new artwork, books and decorative objects. Score a fresh outlook for your efforts.

A new place to live may incorporate a special meditation room for your new mental affirmations, a pretty aspect, a romantic garden, a shrine, a great new location and ... (best thing of all) potentially great new neighbors!

Energy clearing in an existing physical space is one of the best methods I know to bring in new energy. Vacuuming, rearranging objects and furniture, cleaning, dusting and paring down excess stuff are tremendously therapeutic activities. And if you have never heard of the principles of feng shui, now is a great time to find out. Borrow a book on the subject from your local library or buy one (there are tons in book stores) so you can check out your best directions and the advantages of maximizing ch'i. Remember: it's all about energy. Let it flow! It may sound bizarre, but if cleaning up requires a lot of energy, it gives you even more.

SPRUCE UP THE LOVE CORNER
IN YOUR HOUSE AND, WHILE
YOU'RE THERE, CHECK OUT
ALL THE OTHER CORNERS TOO.
YOU NEVER KNOW WHAT YOU
MIGHT BE ABLE TO MANIFEST.

39

Lovesick?

The symptoms and the cure

But what if you can't get off the couch because you can't? Well let's deal with that then. The fact? You're lovesick. And in this state you do feel literally sick. Your mind is telling your body that things are definitely not OK. Your body is responding to the news that your ideal partner for life no longer thinks you're their ideal partner for life, for who knows how many reasons, and so it's gone out in sympathy with your tortured mind. But there it is and you are now in the throes of gut-wrenching agony with physical symptoms to match your emotional ones. Great. It's not unusual in the initial days after a breakup to feel as though you can barely function. The physical checklist might go something like this:

* No appetite or too much
* Can't sleep or you can't stop sleeping
* Feel exhausted the whole time
* Can't speak or have difficulty communicating
* Cry all the time or on-and-off crying jags
* Headaches
* Bowel problems
* Panic attacks and feelings of anxiety
* Want to throw up from the stress
* Flu-type symptoms but it's not the flu

That is a general list of the worst of the symptoms. You may have any number of these depending on the day or how long it has been. The symptoms may come in waves. They are the symptoms of grief. Feelings of anger are commonly in the mix too (just to make things even more complex!). These symptoms also mirror the effects of depression, although depression can involve other more intense emotional and psychological symptoms: hopelessness and a general feeling that your life is a disaster; a lack of energy or enthusiasm for anything; or feelings of suicide. As mentioned above, if these are the overwhelming feelings, then you definitely need to enlist outside help.

Grief occurs in stages,

as was originally said by Elizabeth Kubler-Ross in relation to dying, we tend to move through some identifiable stages in response to loss:

Shock
the facts/change in situation

Denial
the barriers/protection of

Depression
the loss/(emotional pain)

Anger
the reactions/processing

Bargaining
the negotiation/forgiveness

Acceptance
the resolution/release

At any moment you may go back and forward through any of these, but they're all part of the cycle of grieving.

Sometimes there may be aftershocks too. For example, your partner delivers news that they wish to be single and then (soon) after that comes the news that they have found a new relationship. To top that (as if it couldn't get worse) they are now getting married (it can), and then you hear, months after, that they are about to become a parent (final straw). Now that may be an exaggerated and speeded-up view of events but each time a piece of news (another one of 'the facts') comes in, a new cycle of grieving can be triggered. This is because your own dreams, hopes and expectations are being systematically dismantled over a period of time. No matter which leg of the cycle you are on, it can be extremely demanding on your psyche and your body. You can let yourself off the mood swings though, and here's how.

THE CURE

The Home Breakup Cure starts with:

1 Lots and lots of mineral
water and herbal teas

2 Equal amounts of
fresh air

3 A new routine for your body:
yoga, Pilates, exercise, sport

4 Vitamins (especially Vitamin C,
magnesium, and B vitamins)

5 Really healthy food, preferably
organic and definitely not junk

6 More sleep and herbal supplements
to help you if you're up all night

7 Other supplements — St Johns Wort,
Rescue Remedy, natural mood enhancers

8 Massage to help
loosen up tension

9 Meditation to
clear the mind

These will be explored in more detail later in this chapter. But at
least now you have the basic checklist!

Stressed?
Time for a nice cup of tea, dear...

One of the most underrated cure-alls for any sort of crisis is to make a good old cup of tea. It might sound old-fashioned, and it is. But old remedies do work — that's why they're old!

Herbal teas can be very soothing. They work on your central nervous system to calm and balance it. Try peppermint, jasmine, lemongrass, infuse green tea with ginger (very cleansing for your liver, the seat of anger), rosehip and chamomile. Add a teaspoon of organic honey if it's hard to get used to the taste. The main thing is to avoid caffeinated drinks such as colas and coffee at this time. These drain the adrenal glands and when you are under stress that's already happening to the max. Give your glands a break! Be a natural hippy chick and go herbal instead.

Danger ahead
the side-effects of breaking up

If your relationship breakup is leading you down the alleyway to the (dark) amusement hall of substance abuse, now's the time to turn back. Any drugs or alcohol will only make things worse, even if you are able to convince yourself that they are helping to get you through it (that's called 'being in denial'!). On the contrary, they are holding you back. They are adding further toxins and stress to your overloaded system and they will mess with any clarity you may have on your situation. It's a guarantee that you will regret it. Plus, under their influence you are more likely to behave in a way that won't make you happy in the morning. Need I list here the perils and pitfalls of hangovers, casual sex (if you're not mentally and physically prepared), come-downs, not to mention the possibility of ending up in a seriously risky/heavy scene? This is a time to be really gentle with yourself and protect yourself, and any substance abuse will only play havoc with your recovery. Plus, it will expose you to further depression after the effects have worn off. And that's a well-documented fact.

DON'T TAKE DRUGS OR DRINK EXCESSIVE AMOUNTS OF ALCOHOL

THIS IS THE TIME TO: BE CLEAR HEADED AND LOGICAL, BE CALM AND CONTROLLED, BE AT YOUR BEST, NOT YOUR LOWEST, STAY FOCUSED, BE CAREFUL, BE VIGILANT, GO FOR THE NATURAL HIGH OF GOOD HEALTH, BE REWARDED. BIGTIME.

Get thee to the doctor! Time for a checkup

If things get emotionally intense (say you're going back and forth with your ex and it's beyond what you can cope with) and physically you're falling apart as a result, it's time to get to a doctor and get an expert overhaul. Doctors can understand exactly what's going on for you and they know what you need. Sometimes it's a necessary intervention — even if only to get you through the week. Don't struggle on by yourself, help is as close as the nearest clinic. If you plan to do the detox below (which I recommend only under supervision of a parent or doctor) then it's a good idea to have a checkup first anyway. Make yourself your priority project and start from square one. Be healthily selfish now.

RECOVERY DETOX FOR YOUR BODY

With all the free radicals running around your body due to stress, you need to be on top of your detox program. Don't desert your poor old body and make it work harder than it needs to by giving it stuff that will only make it sluggish (read: all prepackaged snacks, sweets or junk food!). Your body needs you to be on top of things now more than ever! **CUT DOWN:** on all the following items for a week: red meat, dairy products, coffee, tea (unless decaffeinated), colas, soft drinks, refined sugar and glucose products, yeast-based food such as breads and pasta, products which are high in salt (soy sauce, crisps), all forms of alcohol. Give your system a break. Feel your mood and energy lift accordingly. **DRINK:** The trick to the whole thing is water, water and more water. Try for a minimum of two liters and a maximum of four. It may seem like a lot, but you'll not only have glowing skin for your efforts, the water will also filter all the toxins through your kidneys, which will be working well once they are properly hydrated. **EAT:** fresh organic fruit in the form of different types of berries (great for Vitamin C), apples, oranges, bananas (potassium) and, if you can get them, tropical fruit such as papaya, pineapple and mangoes. Think fructose (fruit-based sugar) not sucrose (including refined or artificial sugars and sugar substitutes). **SQUEEZE:** vegetables into juices: celery, carrot, beet, ginger, zucchini, parsley. **RELAX:** Kick back and let your body do some of the letting go for you.

THE HEARTBREAK RECOVERY EATING PLAN

The Detox Program is the starting block so you can lay a new, healthier food foundation for your new phase. Once you've detoxed, you cut down the cravings you may have for the foods on the baddies list (see previous page). Switch to this way of eating and you'll never look back. **It's the simplest thing ever:** you get to eat exactly what you want because you want only healthy food, and that's exactly what your body needs. So you trick your body into always wanting healthy food and that's why a detox can be a great booster. **FACT:** You need to eat much more than you think and right now, probably more than you feel like. But there's no need to force anything. You'll see that it comes naturally, once you begin. **Hold the positive belief:** all you are going through is going to benefit you in many ways, from here on. If you treat your body well, your mental and spiritual recovery will be boosted to another level.

yum!

Go light!

Eat heaps of green salads, steamed vegetables, pasta and brown rice (for energy), tofu/soy products such as tempe. You can't overdo it! Eat fish raw in the form of sushi and sashimi, which are light and filled with essential fatty acids, or eat grilled, baked or steamed fish. When you're sick to death of herbal tea and water, miso soup is a handy (and necessary) alternative. The live enzymes in miso soup pack a punch.

SEVEN SIMPLE STEPS TO POSITIVE EATING:

1 Mornings: fruit salad and soy yogurt or yeast-free sourdough toast with sliced strawberries or bananas and soy yogurt topping

2 Lunch: green salads with light olive oil dressing, a tin of tuna, tomatoes and garlic

3 Light lunch alternative: sushi/sashimi box with miso soup

4 Pre-dinner snack: low-sodium crackers with dip, such as hummus (chick pea dip) or guacamole (avocado dip), yogurt–cucumber dip, mix with papadams, raw almonds and unsalted peanuts, plain corn chips and unsalted salsa dip.

5 Dinner: tempe, tofu, grilled fish or lamb with steamed vegetables or mixed salad

6 Between meals: fruit or the occasional glass of freshly squeezed fruit juice for a quick energy boost

7 Drinks: WATER WATER WATER, herbal teas, miso soup, vegetable juice

The key to getting with the program is vitamins. For this part of the plan, I absolutely recommend you see a naturopath first and if you don't have a naturopath consult your doctor before you go shopping! It can be a costly and wasteful exercise to buy copious quantities of supplements if you don't really know what you're doing. It's all very well to have expensive urine, but there is a school of thought that says too many vitamins can stress your system out. It's truly buyer beware! Personally I am with the moderate school that says take a few basic supplements to replace water-soluble vitamins and get most of your good stuff direct from mother nature in the form of good (organic where possible!) food. **Anything you take or eat alters your body chemistry.** Suffice to say Vitamin C, B complex, magnesium, and a good all-round multivitamin will support the other good stuff you're doing for your body! There are many excellent books by qualified naturopaths. Leslie Kenton is one of my favorites and her books are international bestsellers. She has a strong spiritual yet wonderfully practical approach to the mind–body connection. **A note about your body chemistry.** In *The Love Survival Kit*, there is a section on the alchemy of letting go. The basic idea is that we 'fuse' our auras with another person when we hang out with them a lot, so when they are not there (especially if it has been a very strong connection) the lack of their presence causes 'withdrawal symptoms'. It's yet another reason why splitting up with someone can be so unbearably painful. This will be further explored in the SPIRIT section. I mention it here because doing the right things for your body now will assist your spirit to mend.

Body chemistry lessons

— VITAMINS R U

Laugh — it's the best therapy ever

One of the most effective ways to get a new vibe going is to get truckloads of comedies from your local video store. That way, if you insist on remaining on the couch or in bed, you'll be laughing hard while you're there. Which has to beat crying! Romantic comedy (funny as opposed to sentimental), back-to-back with stand-up comedy is a certain cure-all. You can't beat Eddie Murphy, Jim Carrey and even Austin Powers for total distraction. They tell the hilarious and ridiculous side of being lovelorn. Of being human! And that can't be a bad thing. The more you can view things in YOUR life as hilarious and ridiculous, the faster you'll be on the way to a complete recovery. Stock up on books too — you can't beat great fiction for transporting you to another world of someone else's heartache and guarantee-ing you forget about your own.

57

Aromatherapy
you're on the right scent

LOOKS LIKE, SMELLS LIKE, MUST
BE A ... BROKEN HEART!

Aromatherapy is another tool in your
breakup survival and recovery kit.
Burning essential oils in a water-
based oil burner or adding these
to massage oil (such as almond or
jojoba oil) can be a brilliant way
to soothe and relieve your fraught
nervous system and calm you down.
Always keep a bottle of lavender
essential oil handy, it reduces tension
and anxiety even if you just take the
occasional whiff straight from the
bottle. Vanilla and jasmine are also
calming. Citrus-based oils such as
orange, mandarin and lime will rev
you up and get you motivated.

WORKING OUT IS AN ESSENTIAL TOOL TO RECOVERY. THERE'S NOTHING LIKE BEING PHYSICALLY EXHAUSTED TO LOSE EMOTIONAL AND MENTAL BAGGAGE.

Let's take a look at your overall fitness strategy...
Even if you loathe exercise, you can do a lot to help this entire program (and your own cause) by moving! Walking is great — get headphones, a slamming CD or tape and get out there. Running and swimming work too. Combine these with some light resistance work for a total body workout. You know the drill: push-ups, sit-ups, tricep dips, squats, lunges and you'll already put some pep in your step. Sport of any kind is another great tension reducer: tennis, surfing, golf, skateboarding, rollerblading or sailing. Team sports such as basketball get you focused on a group goal. But the key to really getting stress out is the gym. Pump iron — free and fixed weights are great mood lifters. Maybe it's time to book a session with a personal trainer (love an expert!) and give them a specific brief of what you'd like to achieve. Add to this gym routine some yoga and some less goal-oriented activities like bushwalking and windsurfing or even just bodysurfing for fun, and you have a balanced plan.

Fit 4 love & life

YOGI FOR HIRE ...
GET ON YOUR MAT AND GET HIGHER

With the current worldwide yoga explosion (thanks Madonna), we have the world's most ancient form of exercise for the mind, body and spirit available in practically every community hall or local gym. Yoga reigns supreme as a force for reshaping you on every level. It's an incredibly powerful support system for the new and changing you. The 'Salute to the Sun' is a simple and effective ritual that can be performed upon rising and there are other more elaborate routines that can be learned. Yoga is a LEARNING portal for unity of mind, body and spirit. It's a physical way to shift your attention away from your head and into your body and soul.

Massage Magic ...
Healing Hands

There is nothing quite like a good, deep massage to rejuvenate the senses and calm the mind — not to mention the various aches and pains you will undoubtedly have after all this activity! Massage is a healthy, neutral way to be touched and have contact with others, especially if you've been feeling alienated or isolated.

The benefits of massage are legendary:

* increased circulation
* reduced stress and tension
* relaxed muscles (that were cramped and knotted)
* general pain relief and healing
* younger-looking skin
* a much better (read: blissed out) mood

Massage is an essential part of any healthy lifestyle, as important as good food and fresh water. The benefits of massage can be instant and far-reaching.

Sleep

and more sleep:
your rest and recovery strategy

Sleep, sleep and more sleep.

The more z's in the bank you have, the better you'll cope with the waking hours. Pick a time to sleep and a time to rise. Make it regular and stick to your routine. It's your time to dream.

Because...

you're not a machine!

zzzzzzzzzzZ...

JUST
REMEMBER
TO
BREATHE...

The
balancing act
within

It's all about your body chemistry fighting for balance under duress — mind, body and spirit must be in balance for total harmony and unity. If one of these is out of whack the others are thrown out. All three out of balance and you have ...

chaos!

DO THE RIGHT THINGS
TO SUSTAIN YOUR
BODY AND YOU'LL
BE ABLE TO HANDLE
ANYTHING — EMO-
TIONALLY, PHYSICALLY,
MENTALLY AND SPIR-
ITUALLY — THAT GETS
THROWN YOUR WAY.
YOU HAVE TO TAKE
CHARGE AND NOT LET
YOUR MIND OR YOUR
BODY 'RUN' YOU.

all in your head. It's all in your head. It's all in your head. It's all in your head. It's all in

your head. It's all in your head. It's all in your head. It's all in your head. It's all in your he

MIND OVER MATTER

It's all in your head!

The aftermath of any relationship breakup is a good opportunity to check out the mysterious workings of your own personal computer — the one that's on top of your shoulders, that is! If you've been stuck in a rut relationship-wise or perhaps just stuck in general, you may need a change of software. If things are really chaotic 'in there', you might have to check out your hard-wiring too, but that's a taller order. For that major kind of overhaul you may need some extra help and support in the form of counseling or ongoing therapy to get you there.

REMEMBER, IF YOU OR A FRIEND ARE SUFFERING FROM DEPRESSION AND HAVE THOUGHT ABOUT DOING HARM TO EITHER YOURSELF OR OTHERS, YOU NEED TO GET PROFESSIONAL SUPPORT AND HELP AT THIS TIME.

But wherever you find yourself, be kind to yourself now. You deserve it. It's also useful to keep this in mind: there are many variables (infinite, actually) at work in your own head and some have played a part in whatever happened regarding your relationship. And there are just as many variables in your ex-partner's mind. The mental variables each of you have brought to your relationship become critical in the event of a breakup and pretty much dictate how you each handle things (move on, that is) from that point.

When you really think about it (and I'm sure you will), with all the variables in play, it's incredible that we get relationships off the ground at all!

be kind to

yourself now

Hook, line and ...

The starting point of moving on is letting yourself off the hook: ta-da! Nothing you can do or say can change the way things are now. It's not your fault. For goodness' sake don't go through the 'if onlys'. By this I mean...

* If only I was prettier/funnier/skinnier/richer/smarter/
  _____ (fill in the blank)
* If only he hadn't met her/him/them
* If only we had moved in together
* If only I could make him change his mind
* If only I hadn't trusted him/her/them
* If only I had done x
* If only I hadn't said y
* If only z hadn't happened
* If only they didn't know that ... etc. etc. etc.

Well, you get the general idea. The possibilities are infinite. And even if you could list them all, it would get you nowhere fast. The point is you can't control everything. Bottom line ... it's no one's FAULT ... it's a sign from the Universe that there is soul work to be done, by one or both of you.

How's that for a radical new perspective? That's right, let's just put it back to the good old Universe!

... floater

STOP BLAMING YOURSELF
AND THEN YOU CAN STOP BLAMING YOUR EX

Now if this sounds vague and less than helpful, here are a few more specific scenarios for you to contemplate. For example, you may be self-sabotaging:

** Do you believe you are a lovable person?

Do you believe you deserve to have a happy relationship?

* Do you really want to be in a relationship?

Perhaps you have self-esteem problems that you tend to project onto your partner, like a basic insecurity about your own value as a person. If so, this may lead to fears that eventually undermine your relationships. Or perhaps a lack of self-esteem means you're afraid to be alone, even temporarily, so you haven't been able to get a clear view of what you want and end up in sub-standard relationships. Or perhaps you're inexperienced with the level of relationship intensity. Or they are. Or maybe your partner is just a low-down, rotten scoundrel! Or all of the above. These things are all about what's in our heads, and can cause relationship problems! But where there is a conscious will to do so — primarily yours, that is — these things can change.

NOW IS YOUR CHANCE TO TAKE CHARGE ... CONSCIOUSLY!

The main thing you need for good relationships is a sense of your self, so you have very clear boundaries and a strong iden- tity. This allows you to 'hold firm' when things get a bit turbulent and it means that you are never compromised. Relationships are not about 'becoming' another person to please someone else. Relationships are designed to help you 'become' yourself. All relationships are perfect vehicles to help you do this.

Relationships show you who you are and that's why they are often so fraught with problems and tension. Finding out who you are involves checking out your own shadow side too and this can be heavy-duty. For each person involved. But there is an upside. If you take responsibility for the problems — whether it's your stuff or theirs — you might have set yourself up for a challenge but you have also positioned yourself perfectly for personal growth. And that is the real prize, no matter what the circumstances that led to it. Relationship breakups show you where you need to do the work.

91

All relationships will expose either one or both of you.

92

Remember,
life is about one thing:
It's ALL about
your personal growth!

You and Your Destiny

For those of you who have been reading *girlosophy* for a while you know that one of the themes of the books is that you (and your soul) have a personal mission — your destiny. Figuring out yourself is the key to figuring out your destiny and this can cause many of us a lot of pain throughout life. It can be hard. It can feel like work. But however hard it may seem, it's all about your 'soul life' while you're here.

WHO ARE YOU? IT'S THE KEY QUESTION...

95

The great news about this is that no experience, good or bad, goes to waste! Everything we experience, whether it's generated by us or not, leaves an imprint on our soul.

Experiences equal knowledge gained. They are part of the evolution of your SELF.

Reflecting on past experiences benefits each of us, but you will need to make time to do so. Sometimes the best time to work on yourself is when you're not in a relationship. Being single gives you more time to think! Growth can occur more freely and more spontaneously when it's unfettered by others. The breakup of a relationship may signal that you are ready to assimilate your experiences and do some more soul work.

A BREAKUP IS A SIGNAL FROM THE UNIVERSE THAT IT'S TIME FOR YOU TO CONCENTRATE ON YOU.

And in any case, that will be required of you after a certain point in life or when you're in a 'next-level' relationship, such as a marriage or living with a partner permanently. By 'next-level' I mean that you have to work on your stuff individually and at the same time balance that with another person, who is (or should be) doing the same. That's quite a balancing act! Two people growing together while they are developing as individuals is full-on! And that's why these kinds of relationships are the ultimate test.

And then there's the ultra-gnarly question...

SO WHERE DOES
THAT LEAVE ME NOW?

Hmmm. Back to how you're feeling:

You are ... single, alone, solo, estranged, deceived, dumped, ditched, disillusioned, brokenhearted, disenchanted, depressed, disheartened, disbelieving, in denial ... or all of the above.

But no matter what: YOU HAVE TO FACE THE FACTS AND DO THE HARD YARDS NOW ... IT'S OVER.

girlo

There are probably many labels that could describe where you find yourself right now. You are staring pain and reality in the face! But labels can be limiting. DITCH THE LABEL! Labels usually don't describe the reality of each person's individual situation. They may describe the phase you're in, but really labels are just words. This is the secret: in matters of the heart, your mind can mess you up! In order to get to the heart of the matter — and in particular to your own heart — you need to delve into your mind. To delve is to dig deep. Sounds daunting? Well, yes it can be, but this is the best starting point for your full recovery in the aftermath of any relationship breakup.

100

Mind your own business

By 'mind' I mean your entire conscious (and often secret) inner world. This includes your mental attitudes and any thoughts you may have about your relationship, your ex-partner (and his/her predecessor/s), the cause of the breakup, and, most importantly, about yourself. Now you're single, you're ideally placed to begin to think in new ways and see new possibilities.

CHANGE THE SOFTWARE,
BUT CHECK OUT THE HARDWARE TOO...

You will need to examine some of the thoughts that have (no doubt) been going around in a non-stop loop in that overworked brain of yours (the hardware). The software can be described as the current story you are running and any baggage you may carry with you as a result of your past. Your basic set-up emotionally and mentally comes from all the experiences you have incorporated since you were a child. When it comes to relationship drama of any kind, you need to figure out the reasons, see the patterns and come to conclusions so you can get up and going again with confidence. It can be scary at certain times, I'll grant you. But no guts, no glory.

Not every breakup needs major analysis, even if it is painful. You may have chosen your partner unwisely and may be able to see clearly the reasons why it wasn't meant to be. Now you're grieving and letting go of the attachment without needing massive rewiring. But if a lot of karma is involved (see the SPIRIT section for the discussion of karma), or if the situation is intensely loaded, you will need some powerful tools to sift through the debris and get to the crux of the matter.

If you are finding it hard to break your thought patterns — in other words, you find yourself going over and over the same conversations, scenarios and situations, but there's no change in your conclusions or analysis — then you're in a big rut. And you must try to climb out of it. You could give yourself a time limit for going over the relationship and then, sticking to the date, try to stop thinking about it. The other thing to do is to step back and acknowledge that you're in a loop and that you have to — need to! — change the pattern. Therapy or counseling can help here — friends can only say so much, no matter how much they love and support you.

After a certain amount of time, you need to get off the loop. After a certain amount of time, you need to get off the loop. After a certain amount of time, you need to get off the loop. After a certain amount of time, you need to get off the loop.

Loop.

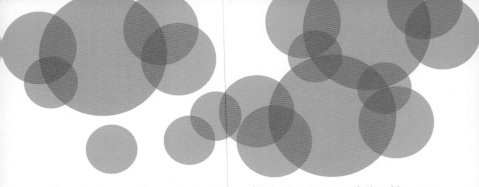

If you find yourself repeating patterns of behavior, or your relationships seem to run the same course over and over, then you might need to sort out a few issues. You know you're stuck in a pattern when different partners end up being so similar, and you break up for the same reasons each time with different people. You're running to a script and you need to change it. This is what I call 'checking out the hardware'.

WHAT'S THE ANSWER THEN?

Replace your negative thoughts with positive affirmations (see Affirmations in SPIRIT) and be vigilant about 'canceling' negativity with positive thinking. Each time you think something negative, replace it with its exact opposite — the positive. And repeat the positive. It takes a lot to cancel a negative thought — they can be powerful, so you need to disarm them through repetition.

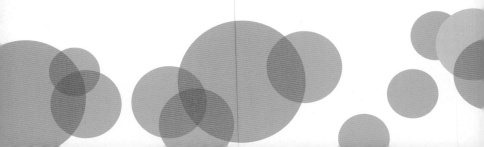

THE OTHER ANSWER IS ...

TAKE ACTION.
AND DO IT NOW.

Go massive not passive!

Because you can't just flick a switch on these things, one thing that really helps is to get out of your head and get into your body instead. That's right, by following the advice in the BODY chapter, you're going to become a power walker, a marathon runner, a surfer, a dancer, a yoga devotee, a swimmer, a tennis player, a windsurfer, a skateboarder, a Pilates expert, a bushwalker ... anything that gets you physical and gives your poor overworked mind some distractions. Exercise helps to get some order into the mind. Call it an enforced meditation if you like! It'll force your mind to focus on your muscles instead of on negative thoughts.

The truth? Wallowing might work, but only in the short term.

At some stage (and the sooner the better) you have to get off the couch or out from under that doona and get going again. Even *Legally Blonde*'s Elle Woods (a fave girlo breakup survivor) could only eat chocolates in bed for so long. **[Note for movie buffs:** she was also nice to her rival who ended up being her best friend after dumping the dreaded Warner!]

It helps if you have a plan and the best plan is one that involves doing something that is purely for yourself, not based on a suspect agenda to get someone back. The kind of plan we're talking about is one that gets you revved up and motivated, feeling great and interested in the world around you. That's what's going to get you out of bed and onto the next stage.

But how long will it take? However long it takes is how long it takes ... and how long you need. Some people bounce back from everything with a bit of time, while others just need more. Time is the only thing in this life that is non-negotiable.

And you won't want to hear this, BUT ...
TIME HEALS EVERYTHING.

Honestly, it really does.

What kind of work do you have to do?

It will be easier to move on with things if you begin to do the real work of sorting through the lessons. The old maxim 'Time heals everything' applies, but ... time is as time does. That's why time is best left to its own devices while you get very busy and productive. The thing is, you'll have to do a bit of work to get into the core stuff, process it, learn it and then you will be offered a new opportunity in the form of a new relationship or interaction. Think of it this way: it might be disastrous to meet someone right away if you haven't done the work and you're not ready/clear/healed/emotionally stable. You may miss the REAL PRIZE. Or worse, stagger into a situation similar to the one you've just come out of. The sort of work that you've probably been avoiding! You may need to 're-wire' your mind regarding the choices you have been making. Or you may simply need to pinpoint where you ignored some key intuition early on. Think about why you behaved in a certain way or did certain things or perhaps why you CHOSE to ignore something — a piece of information that came to you out of the blue, a feeling, an observation — that was only there to help you. Why do you choose the same types of partners only to be disappointed over and over? Why do you rebel by choosing to be with someone your family definitely would not like or who wouldn't fit in, if that is really important to you? Why do you become neurotic and needy in a relationship? These are big questions that are worth thinking about carefully. Or do your partners want to cramp your style or control you in some way? Then you have to ask yourself and them, why? Chances are they'll fudge an answer to keep you from guessing the truth. But if you have been or are in a situation like this, then you must understand that in some way it was or is, serving you. Even in a negative way. Hmmm.

Basically, you don't feel (deep down) that you deserve better. This realization is the clue to the work we've been talking about.

What you learn about yourself now will be invaluable for your future. This is the silver lining to focus on. The Universe works to help us all, albeit more often than not in mysterious ways. A bit of recapping and you may find that certain choices you have made no longer serve you as they were based on old assumptions you hold about yourself and relationships in general. Perhaps you are hamstrung by what your family or parents have told you or their fixed opinions of what you are like. Maybe they (shock, horror!) don't always know what's best for you. Long held assumptions may need to go out the window. Sometimes, it's better to start from scratch. Fresh is best! **Make some new lists, for instance:**

A what you have learned about yourself; and

B what you have been used to doing in the past; plus

C what you might like to do differently in the future; and therefore

D what you now want for your next relationship; and/or

E what you now want for the next stage — you don't have to want a relationship at all.

It can get tough but this is the time to knuckle down and get all that stuff you've had whirling around like candy floss out of your head and onto the table so you can see what's what. Painful? Quite often, yes, and confusing too, but hopefully only in the short term if you can 'gut it out'. Examining your thoughts, past and present, is the only way you'll be able to see how you got where you are — for better or worse. In this way, you can take what you need from your past in order to reinvent yourself into the future.

Clear the mental decks and see what new stuff comes your way...

MEDITATION WORKS WONDERS:
THE WAY IN IS YOUR WAY OUT!

The question 'What is the nature of mind?' has kept scholars, philosophers and spiritualists going for centuries so it's a safe bet I can't give you the answer here. However, as a fellow girlosopher who's 'been there', what I can tell you is this: no matter what the situation appears to be, the whole thing is all in your mind. So, having said that, let's get into it. What's been in or on your mind?

Let's start by making a general list.

Perhaps in the period before the end of the relationship ...

* You were insecure about a few things — say, your looks or image
* You were wondering why he didn't spend more time with you
* You were jealous of the other people he was spending time with — male or female
* You weren't sure if he felt about you the way that you felt about him
* You wanted constant reassurance about his feelings for you
* You needed a lot of his attention
* You constantly wanted to know where the relationship was 'going'
* You were not sure if being in a relationship was what you wanted
* You had been thinking about other people ... even in a passing way
* You believed it was always more about what he wanted and his needs
* You had been projecting into the future rather than simply enjoying the present
* You found yourself thinking about him all the time even when he was with you
* You wanted to change things about your life but didn't know exactly what

And that's just for starters! There are infinite possibilities — these are just some of the more obvious ones. Now, to find out where your head is at, grab a piece of paper and write down the thoughts you had during your past relationship. It helps if you do this after a mini-meditation. Clear your mind of daily clutter (see the classic girlo Meditation guide at the back of the book). You can even work on other past relationships if you can remember the specifics.

You can change
anything about yourself
if you truly want to.

IF YOU HAVE MADE
DECISIONS AND EVEN
TAKEN TENTATIVE STEPS
TOWARDS CHANGE THEN
YOU'LL SOON BE IN GREAT
SHAPE TO MANIFEST WHAT
YOU REALLY WANT. THIS
IS A GREAT EXERCISE FOR
UNCOVERING PATTERNS
THAT MAY BE CAUSING
YOU PROBLEMS IN RELA-
TIONSHIPS AND FIGURING
OUT WHAT YOU WANT TO DO
— OR WHAT YOU WANT TO
HAPPEN — THE NEXT TIME.

YOU'LL GET IT RIGHT (OR YOU'LL GET CLOSER) THE NEXT TIME

What I know for sure: it helps to get things out of your head and onto paper.

You've been true to HIM but have you been true to YOU?

YOU NEED TO LOOK
AFTER YOURSELF

Looking after yourself —
being healthily selfish

means having clear boundaries. Having clear boundaries means knowing what your own code is and sticking to it, especially when someone acts in ways that show they do not respect you. Too much emphasis on others and what they may or may not be thinking (and you can never know for sure) is as unbalanced as too much emphasis on yourself. The trick is to find the middle ground — and this is an art form — that only comes with practice and maturity. It's trial and error! Often when things are unraveling in a relationship we find our focus switched entirely to the other person's feelings. What is he/she feeling, as opposed to what am I feeling? That's the exact moment we need to tune back into our own feelings.

YOU ARE RESPONSIBLE FOR YOUR OWN HAPPINESS

Ah-Ha. That old chestnut. And it is true. You can go to a couple of ashrams, into therapy or on a hundred retreats and vision quests, seek advice from every guru from Bali to Bombay but ultimately you will come to this basic realization. It is a foundation belief of Buddhist teaching, and it's also a fact of life!

Here's some advice:
You can't control the way another person thinks
or feels or behaves or develops.

YOU CAN ONLY CONTROL YOURSELF AND YOUR OWN REACTIONS.

It helps if you don't play the 'Blame Game'. Blaming your ex-partner, no matter what they did, won't help you get through the pain barrier or over it faster. Blaming the other person or even a third party (another girl, for example — more on that later) could have quite the opposite effect — it could keep you stuck while you dredge up more ammunition or information to hold your ex fully responsible. Your task is to get on with this new phase of your life.

Relationship Madness:
What happened?

There are so many ways in which breakups occur, that it would be impossible to cover them all here. Let's face it: that's how Hollywood makes its squillions every year! There are as many breakup stories as there are people and relationships, for no two relationships are the same.

The thing to keep in mind is this: someone else is probably going through exactly what you are right now and many others have been through it before you. The experience of a broken heart has fuelled most of the world's great art, and no doubt will continue to do so. It's something we have in common and it's also the reason ... you are never completely alone.

Whatever the specifics, breaking up is a time of madness for all concerned. Luckily it's mostly temporary and often the only bruised thing is an ego or two. However, it is almost always a highly charged time of mixed emotions and sometimes in the confusion, words trip over hearts.

YOU ARE NEVER COMPLETELY ALONE.

Break up in the most constructive way°possible.
One that shows you know exactly what you want.
That's what the Universe is waiting to hear.

Still confused? Make up your own mind!

Often being 'confused' is a smokescreen — on your ex's part. They will say they are confused because they either want something they can't articulate or they want you to articulate something to help them define what they want. Either way it's too much stress for you and is an indication that they need time away to do some sorting. This can sometimes manifest in the 'on-again off-again on-again' relationship. You know you are in this situation when you think you'll go insane if the relationship isn't resolved soon and your parents and friends stop asking you what's happening because they are too nervous to hear the answer. The Solution? It's up to you to set the boundaries and stick to them. There's scant mileage in agreeing to split up and then getting back together the next day with no real resolution or changes. These things need time for any real difference to emerge. You may have to police it — and yourself — to set clear lines for the future of the relationship. If you're a bit hazy there will be no clear direction and things will stay unsettled. It will get you nowhere fast.

The level of energy behind each of these words is often the key to what changed the relationship. Maybe after some time, the balance of power changed (you became more or less independent of your partner) or maybe you shared super-fiery passion between you that couldn't be contained and exploded into fragments. Perhaps career, studies or geography made it impossible to be together. Perhaps your energies were only destined to be combined for a certain time, so you could each learn something as fast as possible before moving forward to your next learning curve.

If you gave the relationship your best and came to it with honest intentions, then you can truly say that you gave it your best shot. Ultimately, this is the most constructive way to view all your relationships, because then they can each play a part in your personal development. They each have their unique beauty and their exquisite moments. The memories are yours alone.

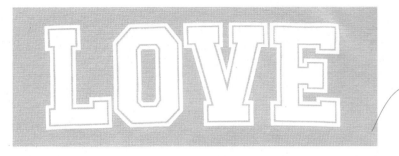

As many have observed, it's not that important who loves you.
What is important is whom you have loved.
That's what shapes you as a person and what truly matters.

LOVE IS RECORDED BY THE UNIVERSE AND FOREVER ETCHED IN THE COSMOS. YOU LOVED. THAT'S THE KEY THING.

EMOTIONS AND COMMUNICATION ...
From A to Z and back again

One of the big questions of a breakup is how much (if any) communication you should have with your ex. As with everything, there are no hard and fast rules here. A lot will depend upon how you feel, how your ex feels, and possibly on other factors such as one of you starting a new relationship or moving away. But once the decision has been made that you are no longer 'together' in a romantic sense, and this has been discussed, then there's really no point in banging on about it. Do yourself a favor — hear or impart the information that is necessary and keep it as calm, sensitive and brief as you can. Perhaps when the dust has settled or when things have changed you can have another conversation.

Even if the split is amicable, it makes it easier on everyone if there is limited or even zero communication for a while. Then, with a bit of breathing space, perspective and healing time, you might even be friends. That's the ideal scenario and unless there have been really serious problems (such as stalking, abuse, addiction or any type of criminal behavior) I encourage you to think about trying to achieve this in the long-term. Just remember, this will probably not be possible immediately, when your feelings are still raw and you haven't fully processed what you might need to. Acceptance and neutrality are not necessarily available to you when you need them most!

It might help you to say something along these lines to your ex.

134

AFTER A RESPECTABLE AMOUNT OF TIME, YOU SHOULD BE ABLE TO STOP GOSSIPING ABOUT YOUR EX, EVEN WITH YOUR FRIENDS.

But if you still have to communicate — let's say you work together, attend the same school or college, see them in your neighborhood all the time — it pays to keep the whole thing as non-emotional as possible when you speak. Try the old PFD approach: polite, friendly and distant. You don't need to tell them every little thing about your life or what you've been up to. You just need to be pleasant, dignified and light. And remember, if you have a new relationship and you're trying to get a reaction to this, then YOU'RE STILL NOT OVER IT. And when you think about it, that sort of behavior is hardly fair to you or your new partner. Do your emotional housekeeping and get your affairs (!) in order and then you'll be able to be happy about whatever happens to each of you.

After a respectable amount of time, you should be able to stop gossiping about your ex, even with your friends. Make a pact that you won't bring the name up ('He-whose-name-shall-not-be-mentioned'). If you do get back together and you've dished the dirt too hard, then you'll look foolish and your friends won't support you. They won't BELIEVE that he's worthy of you if you've gone hardcore on the details! If your friends have only heard your edited version, then they are unlikely to have a balanced opinion. Above all, even if you're only thinking about your ex, do try to be kind about them, even if it's only to yourself. I know it's incredibly hard but … no swearing 'in there' OK? (Oh, and if you do have a temporary lapse, ask the Universe for forgiveness!) Thoughts are pure energy and guess what? The other person can feel them. Everyone can feel how you feel about them, even if you're not in contact directly. We're all psychic you know…

DESIRE AND ER ... THE OTHER WOMAN

This is a tough one. You've been replaced. Maybe there was even a bit of an overlap as your ex ably demonstrated the 'monkey' relationship strategy (ie not letting go of one branch until they had a firm grip on the next one). It makes no difference. There is NOTHING you can actually do if your partner decides to move on to someone new. Absolutely nothing. Except, of course, screaming into a pillow or two until the venom is released and you are spent of energy.

Why would you want to be in a relationship with someone who doesn't want to be in a relationship with YOU?

You can, however, accept the new situation and his new relationship as if you are happy for him. You may feel as though you deserve an Oscar nod for this performance but there is a good reason for it — you're behaving in line with the 'act as if' theory of doing something until it comes naturally. Retreat with dignity. Let him make a mistake, if that's what's meant to happen and then if he comes (crawling) back, then you were right. Or at that point, you can decide if you still want the relation-ship. Or him. Or whatever. No script can be followed here because we're dealing with another person and their desires, which are unfathomable to you and probably even to them! And really what you need to think about is what feels right for you. The point is this: you'll be in the box seat and that means you get to choose. You may decide after consideration to CHOOSE not to be in the relationship. This is a great little trick you can play on your own ego and it's honest — they tell you they've met someone new and on hearing this you decide not to be in a relationship with them — and logical too! It keeps your sense of self somewhat intact and allows you to keep some power in the equation. It may even help you avoid being completely devastated.

You must, however, also let 'the other woman' off the hook.

IT'S NOT HER FAULT AND EVEN IF IT IS, IT'S STILL NOT HER FAULT. SHE'S JUST DOING HER DESTINY. AND HEY, SHE'LL GET SOME LESSONS TOO ... EVENTUALLY. EVERYONE DOES.

If your partner hadn't played their part in forming their new relationship, it would never have happened in the first place. So there is no point in blaming a third person. That will keep you in tissues (and on the couch) for months. And that's definitely not the glorious recovery I have envisaged and planned for you!

BETRAYAL IS A ───────────

No way round it, betrayal sucks. You've been deceived, lied to, ripped off, you've trusted for no good reason and YOU'VE BEEN HAD. Ouch. Best (girlo) way to view it? It's just a sign of the times. Hardcore way to view it? You needed the lesson. It may be that you needed to learn detachment or learn about freedom, or to face other issues such as honesty and integrity. That's a higher way to view it and this is the level of mastery you will hopefully get to. It is my sincerest wish for you that rather than looking at the downside of what has occurred, you'll be more concerned with the overarching issues and what the lessons are for you to absorb.

The problem with fighting a betrayal is that it may become worse for you. It's happened, you've found out or been told by a concerned friend and now … you want revenge. Uh-oh. No stalking his place or incessant phone calls, text messaging or otherwise. Be still. Silence is golden! When you say little or nothing, the message of what you're not saying can have more impact. It's powerful. Put it this way, they know what they've done, so there's no point really 'going there' and letting them have it. You just have to decide what you're going to do with the information.

There's also the possibility that if you carry on too much, you may force your now-ex-partner into staying with someone they don't really want, just because you're behaving so unbearably. Or worse, you may convince your partner into coming back to you because you've made him feel so guilty — not the best reason for a relationship to continue. Or, your behavior in reaction to theirs might be just the reason or excuse they've been waiting for — for whatever reasons. Think about that. To me it shows that everyone needs some time out!

Try dealing with the situation with the five Ds: decorum, dignity, discipline (repeat after me: I will not call anyone names), decency (play fair — you don't want to slum it) and, importantly, detachment.

Let your ex feel insecure about their decision and their desires rather than vindicated because you were a psycho-chick anyway. If they're that committed to being with someone else (and they're obviously not committed to being with you) then nothing you do or say will change their mind.

Everyone is free to make choices. You don't, and can't, own anyone.

YOU DON'T NEED TO EXPOSE YOURSELF TO FURTHER PAIN OR HURT. PROTECTING YOURSELF AND YOUR FEELINGS AND BEHAVING WITH DIGNITY IS YOUR ONLY RESPONSIBILITY AT THIS POINT.

ABOVE ALL, TRY TO OBSERVE IT AS THE UNIVERSE DOES: THIS (YOUR RELA-TIONSHIP AND ITS BREAKUP) IS A SPECK IN THE BLIP OF THE NANOSECOND OF HISTORY'S FART. OR SOMETHING LIKE THAT. IT IS GOING TO SEEM IRRELEVANT AND MEANINGLESS IN THE SCHEME OF THINGS. AND SOONER THAN YOU THINK. YOU'RE BEING GUIDED TO SOMETHING HIGHER, BETTER AND MORE NECESSARY FOR YOUR EVOLUTION.

GIRLO DOUBLE-WARNING:

YOU'RE PROJECTING (UNHEALTHY) AND THEY

MAY BE PLAYING GAMES (DANGER!)

Rejection is...
THE GREATEST APHRODISIAC. OR IS IT?

Clubs (especially nightclubs) operate on this principle! And when it comes to relationships, keeping someone in a state of longing is how some insecure people work. As you get older you'll probably experience this in a number of ways, but hopefully with some savvy as to what it's really about. These people do have psychology on their side — for some ridiculous reason we always want what we can't have — but it's bogus really. Even if it does make the object of desire seem supremely desirable. Some twisted notion that the love of your life is completely 'unavailable' can keep you projecting into what isn't (and can never be) as opposed to what really is possible and meant to be.

The one who says: 'We'll get together sometime in the future, but right now I just want to …
(a) be free
(b) explore this new relationship
(c) be on my own
(d) see what happens
(e) experience other people etc. etc.

That's just serving one thing and one thing only: THEIR EGO. Stay open to the notion that it's a final goodbye and there's someone completely new for you.

Letting go is the ultimate freedom. Hard to do, I know, but very necessary, because this person is actually rejecting you, but trying to keep you there while they do — for reasons best known to themselves. It's called having an each-way bet (that's the nice way to describe it). Putting someone on the old back burner is a classic, but it's a dead end. Perhaps they are doing it because they are really in love with you but they are not ready/not up to it/not — here's the kicker — good enough or not feeling good enough for you (because THEY have low self-esteem). But there's no point thinking about that! In time maybe, but it really is best to let things go so you let in the new. Be on the lookout for the one who rejects you quickly or has an affair while you're together. It might be they don't feel worthy and so they are getting in first — and sabotaging the relationship — just in case you dump them!

Other fish in the sea

Beware the person who wants to keep you dangling.

REASONS TO BE CHEERFUL...
OR AT LEAST TO BE REALISTIC

Your ex was too young / too old / already married / other-wise involved / gay or hetero / illegal / insane / a criminal / a substance abuser / about to be deported ... etc. Any or all of the above reasons lets you off the hook.

This is an easy one. You have been given the perfect 'out' clause. The person you were with was inappropriate or was not meant to be with you long-term and for a good reason (see above). You are being shown carte blanche which allows you — nay encourages you — to move on, pass GO, collect the $200 ... you get the gist. You have to get it, because the Universe is making it really easy for you. The whys and wherefores of the relationship's inevitable breakdown are being clearly spelled out. These are pretty much non-negotiable situations, although as with all scenarios, time can change things. But for right now, the thing is crystal clear.

YOU HAVE TO MOVE ON. Just don't waste too much time wishing things were otherwise. They are what they are. The facts, sadly or not, are the facts.

EACH PERSON IS EXACTLY WHERE THEY NEED TO BE
RELATIONSHIP-WISE FOR A REASON — THE UNIVERSE
KNOWS THE REASONS AND IF YOU TUNE IN TO YOUR
INSTINCT, YOU WILL TOO.

SINGLES vs DOUBLES...
AND IT'S NOT THE US OPEN EITHER

Ah yes. The ultimate sporting challenge: facing center court and being in the spotlight all by yourself. Hmmm. It's a tricky world out there for singles. Don't believe the hype — that singles have it sussed and that all couples think the grass is greener. Often there's a real drought, the landscape is truly brown and everyone knows it! Chances are they think you're having the time of your life, including all the dates/affection/good fun they've foregone now that they're heavily into domestic/mortgaged/full-time love bliss. Chances are you think they're having the coziest, nicest time of their lives including all the invitations/regular physical contact/good couple-kind-of-fun that you can't or won't ever have again. Or even have for the first time, maybe. Of course, none of these assumptions (or fears) are true all of the time or even part of the time. The whole thing is a perception game. And like any game, a strong mental attitude will get you the farthest every time.

Personally I don't really like the word 'single' or perhaps what it implies. Redefining the word and the concept is overdue and necessary in the 21st century. The way I see it, you are on a journey, and part of this journey may be shared with someone else or may be parallel to another person's journey. Or not. You are single your whole life, whether you are in a relationship or not. No one else can get out of bed for you, look after your body for you, eat food for you, think for you … it's all up to you, all the time. Being on your own can be great, but it can also be hard. The truth is, most of us are happier with someone special to share things with. Being without someone can require a lot more of you. You have to find your resourcefulness, your own ability to be positive, to stay strong, have your act together and to do it day in, day out. It's often easier to be in a relationship than willingly take on the grit of daily life alone. However, coping on your own can also show you who you really are and what you are capable of. It can show you the hidden magic of total privacy, the sacredness of solitude and the joy of making decisions for yourself, goal-setting and accomplishment. When you are single and not in a relationship with a 'significant other', it is truly your life.

BEING ALONE MAKES YOU GROW SO WHAT ARE YOU AFRAID OF?

It may indeed be hard being single for a period of time, but it's likewise hard to be in a relationship for a long period of time. And in much the same way that we are polarized in gender as males and females, we are also polarized relationship-wise. There's lots of rubbish written about being on your own (Fun! No responsibility! Parties! Sex!) and there's equal amounts of idealistic crap regarding long-term relationships (Security! Dinner parties! Better Real Estate! Kids!). It seems that for many of us today, the pendulum swings wildly between the two extremes. Surely a better and healthier scenario is one that lands somewhere between the two. We all need to have our freedom. This is crucial. Yet we also need to be able to bounce experience off another and at the same time learn to share and to be compassionate, whilst having the intimacy and growth that come from being in a relationship.

But just in case you're beginning to get all misty-eyed (again!), there is no 'permanent ideal'. And by the way, the tables can turn at any second! Once happily married or together, then, in a nano-heartbeat, happily single or divorced. Or not so happily. The thing is, no one should ever feel smug about their situation or superior (or critical) towards someone else's, because things really do have a habit of changing when you least expect it. The truth is ... NOTHING IS EVER AS IT SEEMS.

So if you've just broken up with someone, this is a time of reevaluation on every level. Now is the perfect time to reappraise exactly what you want to work towards in all aspects of your life. You can rethink your career, where you live, how you dress, your creative outlets, fitness, your social life, a whole host of things. It's this part of being without a relationship that helps you to redefine yourself in a positive and constructive manner.

YOU MAY
CHOOSE TO
BE ON YOUR
OWN. THIS IS
HEALTHY.
LET NO ONE
MAKE YOU
FEEL LESS
BECAUSE YOU
ARE NOT PART
OF A COUPLE.

COMMITMENT MEANS HAVING THE INTENTION NOT TO QUIT

Lack of commitment is quite possibly the most common reason for a breakup. If your relationship or friendship has ended because one of you was unable to commit, then it may be a good thing. If it's not you, it's them! Giving a person time to get their act together so they feel able to go the distance — with YOU — is not just sensible, it's practical. It is far better that they decide to take time out to fix things so they can be in your life properly. And if they're unwilling to try then your relationship has reached its natural conclusion.

You can't force a person to be ready — they are or they're not. And if they tell you they can't give you a commitment, then it's actually in your best interests to believe them. Who needs more pain? It may be the greatest thing they ever do for you. They are being honest! But they must also know that they absolutely risk losing the person (you) that they will not commit to. Risk-taking is a risky business!

Best thing to do? Commit to your own life and be on the lookout for new connections.

FRIENDS AND ENEMIES...
THE FALLOUT

You are bound to experience some change in the social landscape after a breakup. This is to be expected. People can be fickle even when you think they're steadfast. It can come as an unpleasant surprise and then you've got the double-whammy: exes of all types who may appear in places when you aren't expecting to see them. Nightmare! This can have a major impact on your self-esteem. What to do? Chin up. Know that it's THEIR stuff not yours. You can be as nice as possible when necessary and keep your views to yourself. You can allow things to shift however they shift and then see if you still feel the same way about the various people involved. They may swing back your way in time, but who knows ... maybe not. Don't let it faze you. Whoever is in your world right now, is there for a reason and a purpose.

HOW TO COPE? You can decide to minimize your exposure to the chilly new social arena. You can let them act in whatever way they do without plugging into it. You can take it in your stride and react in your own good time. It's a safe bet that a whole bunch of new people are about to enter your life, stage right.

Releasing and allowing, forgiving and flowing. That's the only way to navigate this section of terrain. These changes are part of your destiny.

HOW TO COPE AT SCHOOL OR WORK POST-BREAKUP

More tests — just to see if you have learned your lessons. Going through stuff is hard enough when you're by yourself, but it can be equally challenging to have to be in a group situation when you least feel like engaging with others. Even being with family who are coupled-off can be excruciating (those Christmas dinners!). But sometimes being forced into some sense of normality while you're going through hell can be helpful, as it distracts you from the dreaded 'loop' inside your head and time passes more quickly. Let others know that you're going through a rough patch due to personal reasons (you don't necessarily have to go into specifics), so if you're not your usual bubbly self, that's why. You could tell them that you're on the mend (positive) but it's not easy for you right now (fact). Anyone who is caring does not want to see you suffer and will most likely do anything to get you out of the dumps. School and work can be trying because concentration is hard to maintain and people talk about things that trigger memories. Put the filters on for a while — immerse yourself in your studies, a project, team sports, anything that keeps building your self-worth. You'll feel better for not giving in to the mood swings. And for not giving up.

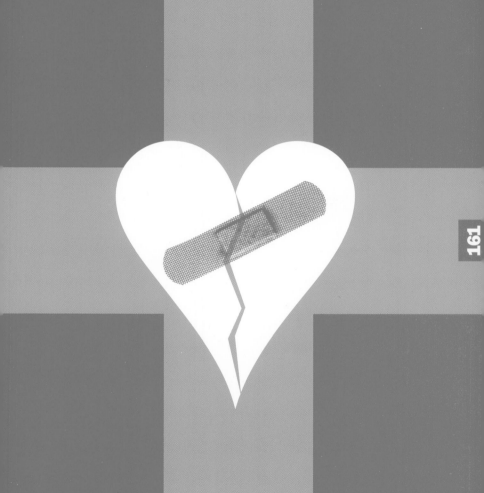

161

WHAT'S ON YOUR MIND IS THE MOST IMPORTANT THING.
REPROGRAM THAT AND YOU WILL SEE INSTANT RESULTS.
THE UNIVERSE WANTS TO GIVE YOU EVERYTHING.
IT WANTS YOU TO HAVE IT ALL.

In this section, we bring it all together ... and work out what it's all about — breaking up, making

up — what the whole thing really meant and why you had to go through it in the first place.

It's all about your soul's journey and how everything you go through can be the making of you as a person.

This chapter is full of concepts that might be hard to wrap your brain around, but once accepted, they will go to the core of you and help you to be comfortable with everything, no matter what happens to you in your life. That's right — everything! In this section we get to the mystical part, the part that's all spirit and energy, which does not necessarily offer a definitive answer to anything. Or need to. This section is about acceptance, harmony, trust and flow. About understanding the perfection in everything as it is, right here, right now. The Universe knows what's best for each of us, at every moment. It's all perfect as far as our soul is concerned. So it's time to honor that.

Your soul's (working) life...

If we have genuine thoughts of compassion and happiness for others, then the Universe rewards us with the same in kind. It's about that simple. So while our soul is hard at work creating and/or burning off karma (more on this later) through our thoughts and actions, we might be coasting through life, blissfully unaware of the cosmic energy we are creating. But, in any event, the relationship (and the breakup) has served our soul in some way.

WHY SOMEONE IS WITH YOU, OR NOT, IS ONE OF THE GREAT UNKNOWNS. LOVE IS THE MAGICAL FORCE IN THE REALITY WE EXPERIENCE WHILE WE'RE ALIVE. FLOWING WITH ITS EBB IS THE THING TO LEARN.

The soul waits for that which is instructive, in order to grow.

It's mind over matter while your soul rolls on...

Tibetan Buddhist monks have a profound question that forms the basis of their lifelong pursuit of enlightenment and that is 'What is the nature of mind?' Well, if you're wondering what on earth Buddhist monks have to do with a relationship breakup and before you even begin to think I've totally lost it — hold on! Spending even a small amount of time thinking about the nature of your own mind will help you with your eventual understanding of yourself and your relationships. And, by the way, Buddhists can teach us loads about all types of relationships. It's the quiet contemplation and discipline of daily meditation that gives them the leading edge here. They understand that the key is ALLOWING someone else to be and do exactly what they need to.

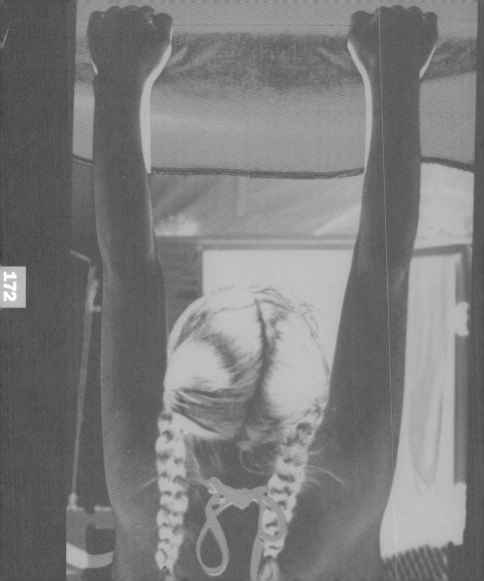

What have you Learned?

No matter what you may think — even if you're right — everyone has to be allowed to make their own mistakes, decisions and moves, and often this won't gel with others who are caught up in them. It may be a huge call to let go, but it's the only way!

WHERE
YOUR MIND IS AT
IS WHERE YOUR SOUL IS
AT! This is why practicing Buddhists spend so much time in meditation, contemplating the nature of their own mind — they know it's the key to their soul's elevation. The less chaos in there, the clearer the thoughts that go out. Clear thinking sends a direct, unfettered beam out to the Universe which only serves to enhance the direct, unfettered response!

Just to recap for those who have not read *girlosophy — A Soul Survival Kit:*

HEARTBREAK IS A PART OF LIFE.

Almost everyone has experienced heartbreak at least once and we each react differently to the breakdown of a relationship. You can help yourself get through it, though, if you take it on in a proactive way:

REALIZE that whatever is happening (or not happening) is part of the grand plan the Universe has divined for your highest good.

DECIDE that you will go through the grief, anger, disbelief and sadness, but ultimately you will recover, having grown, to be wiser.

KNOW that love is infinite and you can generate as much as you consume.

BELIEVE there are no limits to love — and in the future you will love another person and be loved more than you can possibly imagine.

REMEMBER not to be so caught up with crying over a lost skateboard that you miss the Rolls Royce that's parking right in front of you.

YOUR SIXTH SENSE ... YOU ARE PSYCHIC YOU KNOW!

If you think back to when you met your ex, you probably had a sense about things from the very first time you laid eyes on each other. Some people call it love at first sight. Some people call it the sixth sense — your intuition, instinct, a vibe, a feeling ... something that felt different and that told you this was destined. It's a clue from your soul that this is an opportunity for growth. It's your soul going to college! Did you get the lesson? Otherwise you'll go through it again until you do. Your soul will seek out other similar opportunities for you. And that's why looking back on this will give you the understanding and realization that you have fulfilled a part of your destiny. So the thing is, when you are in recovery from a breakup, you need to tune in to what you were meant to learn until you are absolutely certain that you've got it! If only so you don't go through it again.

LOVE AND DESTINY It may sound like a top-40 album but these huge words contain the Universe. And your attitude to each will determine where you find yourself on your life path! Any relationship you are involved in is the 'work-in-progress canvas of your soul figuring out the finished picture. Not everything in your 'faulty relationship' needed to be fixed either. In certain respects all relationships are flawed — and that's because humans are — but they are also, for that very reason, perfect. They are the perfect workshop for the purpose of to learn who we are, and what we need to work on and what we can do with that knowledge. We should simply our individual destiny. In one sense we shouldn't really try to 'work on' our relationships, we should simply just work on ourselves. That's also why a breakup is the perfect time to understand that there are things in life that are not always able to be fixed, nor should they be. A relationship that's ending is often a signal for you to practice the notion of 'let it be'. Only then can you fully appreciate that love is stronger than (and survives) everything.

LOVE & DESTINY:

when your spirit makes another spirit dance

NO ACTION — NO MATTER HOW SMALL — GOES UNNOTICED
OR UNRECORDED BY THE UNIVERSE

KARMA

KARMA IS ACTION.

Those of you who are regular gLrosophy readers will already be familiar with the concept of karma. The word itself means 'action' or 'deed'. The larger concept of karma includes every physical or mental action each one of them when an opportunity arises. Likewise you can't do good things and think negatively. Karma is not as simple as 'if I'm good then I will only have good things happen'. That may be the case but you may also have past karma. If you're going through a difficult period in your life, it doesn't mean you've got 'bad' karma. In gLrosophy's book, it's ALL good, because it's all part of your soul's journey. It could mean that the best is yet to come. Perhaps you're overdue for something really amazing and the Universe is about to give it to you. Puts a new spin on it, doesn't it?

IF YOU WANT TO STEER YOUR WAY THROUGH THE WILDERNESS OF KARMA — AND MOVE PAST THE STUFF THAT OBSCURES YOUR PATH FROM TIME TO TIME — THEN FORGIVENESS IS THE ONLY WAY. IT MAY BE HARD BUT IT IS ABSOLUTELY ESSENTIAL.

FORGIVENESS: THE SHORTCUT THROUGH KARMA

People you are estranged or energetically cut off from will only be free to go when you set them free, by forgiving and releasing them.

Practice saying this, until you really feel it.

I forgive you _____, for not being the person I wanted you to be.
I love and accept all that we have shared as the gifts they are.
I forgive you and release you with love.

It's impossible to say this too often!

The other method is to **'BLESS THE EX'**. This can be a challenge but one that is well worth taking on. It's a beautiful and generous thing to do. And, when you do so, you are also blessing yourself. Even if someone else has been less than generous, it's always a great thing to remain openhearted yourself, even if you still feel angry or hurt. It's the higher course of action — and you know about taking the high road don't you?

BLESS your ex-partner and **ASK** the Universe to send them happiness. Be willing and ready to receive the blessings you deserve in return.

In addition to this, you may wish to **APOLOGIZE** to anyone you may have hurt in the past. Perhaps this was your turn to be on the receiving end for a change! Saying **I'M SORRY** (even if you do this mentally or while you're meditating) is another positive way to heal. It is never too late.

If you are having trouble processing **ANGER**, then a good method is to write down why you are angry and then burn it. And immediately **ASK** the Universe for help in taking the anger away. Pledge that you no longer need anger. It does not serve you in any way and you wish to release it. Do this as often as necessary.

You know
you no
longer have
anger in
your system
when all
you feel is
relief!

THE END MIGHT BE THE BEGINNING

The attachment to what you had, or thought you had, is what's really causing your grief. You are unable to flow, live and therefore love in the present moment.

If you're still struggling, it's because you won't let go of the past — being attached to an outcome is what's messing you up. The only outcome the Universe cares about is your spiritual growth, so it is uninterested in whether you wanted to stay in a particular situation or not. It only cares about your soul's lessons and will let you have what you want if it's truly what you need. By letting go, you never know, you may get the outcome you wanted anyway. That happens a lot!

Cut him/her loose; releasing the attachment. Give yourself peace of mind. Cut the ties that bind. On the other side is

Freedom

SOULMATE, ROOMMATE OR ... JUST A MATE?

Now comes the readjustment part. Perhaps you made a long-term relationship out of someone who might be better in your life as a friend. Or maybe you had a roommate and with the familiarity of living in the same place, you become close. Or perhaps you really have met a soulmate and it's time for you to go your own way until your next soul mission — should you choose to accept it! You can get a lot of satisfaction from keeping a connection and allowing your relationship to take a different form, as long as there's basic understanding and compassion on both sides. It's a wonderful opportunity to demonstrate maturity and keep a friendship. This may only be possible after time has elapsed, but if it's a mutual thing now, you can do it pretty quickly. Your heart needs all sorts of connections and relationships to be satisfied and to experience as much as possible. Different relationships make for a rich soul life — and that's something you need!

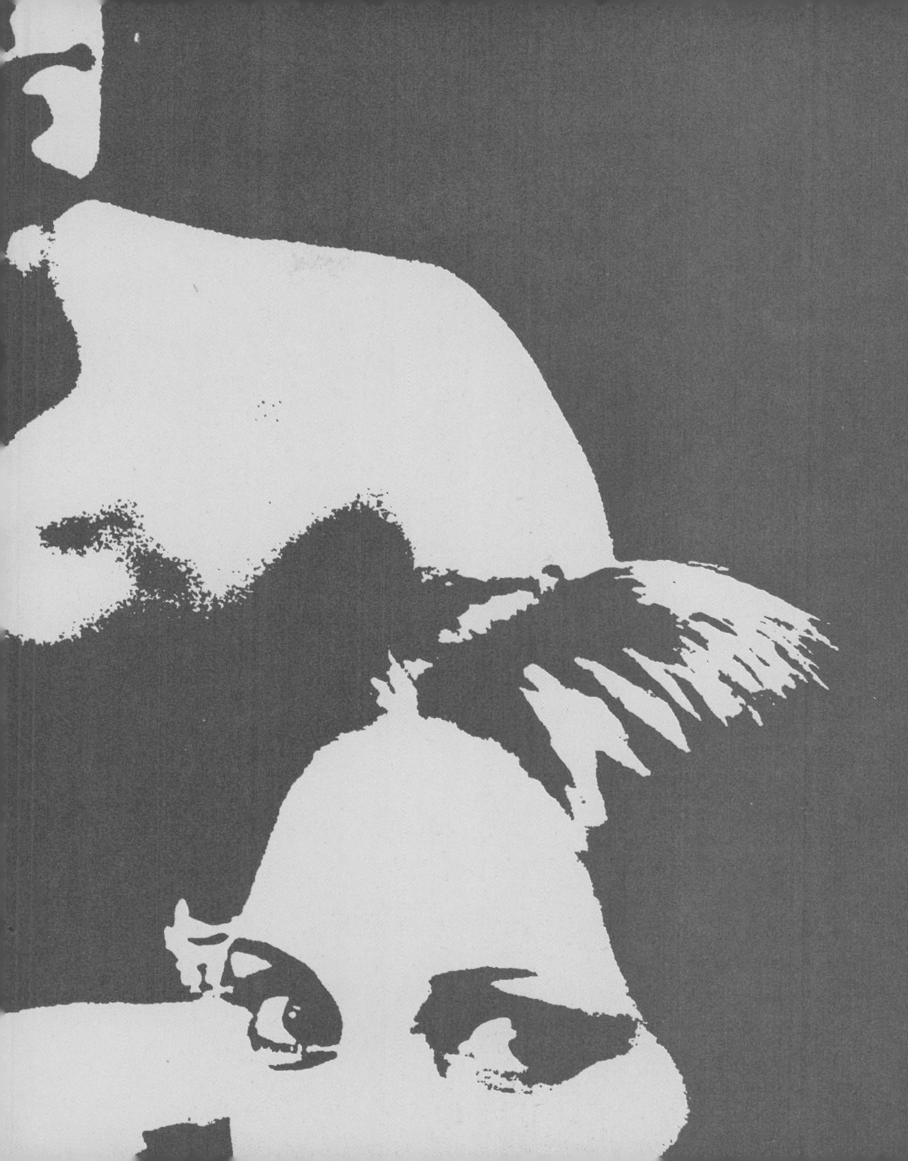

TIME OUT ... FOR PERSONAL REASONS As I've said, you're doing a major overhaul and so it makes sense to give yourself time. Don't jump into a new situation with another person (this is called a REBOUND relationship) or fling yourself in sadness and desperation into the arms of your neighbor, just because you can't bear to be alone. Be a bit selfish and the strength to endure things will come. Consider it a time when you are really focused on yourself. You've been shown a glimpse of freedom and you are priming yourself for the future. Right now, you're taking time out ... for personal reasons.

TAKING YOUR CHAKRAS FOR A SPIN...

Those of you who have *girlosophy* — *The Oracle* will be aware of the details of each of the chakras (you can also find them at the back of this book). Your chakra system is the energy field that is generated by what you're thinking, feeling and doing. It's your cosmic connection to the Universe and it reflects all communication and energy that is going out and coming in. Energy is radiated (in a spinning motion) to and from each of the following areas in your body:

Top of your head, center — **Crown Chakra**
Between your eyebrows — **Third Eye Chakra**
Front of your throat region — **Throat Chakra**
Center of your chest — **Heart Chakra**
Under your rib cage — **Solar Plexus or Power Chakra**
Below your navel — **Lower Abdomen or Sacral Chakra**
Under your pelvis at base of your spine — **Base Chakra**

Chakras make up your cosmic or energy body which reflects exactly what's going on in your real one. They create an aura which is why when you meet certain people you can feel their vibe. That's what chakras do! They are also the energetic keys to healing any imbalance between your mind, body and spirit. Sounds easy? It is really. You can almost always feel when things are not quite flowing in your life and normally this is associated with an illness or a lack of energy or a dull feeling in the associated region. It's therefore crucial to get in touch with each of these energy hotspots, to assist you on your journey to wellness and wholeness. Your heart chakra is the leader of the pack, so when the heart's in turmoil, it can throw the other areas off. Get tuned in to what your heart chakra needs by meditating, reflecting, thinking good thoughts, staying open, being real. Don't spin out!

Crown Chakra

Third eye Chakra

Throat Chakra

Heart Chakra

Solar Plexus Chakra

Sacral Chakra

Base Chakra

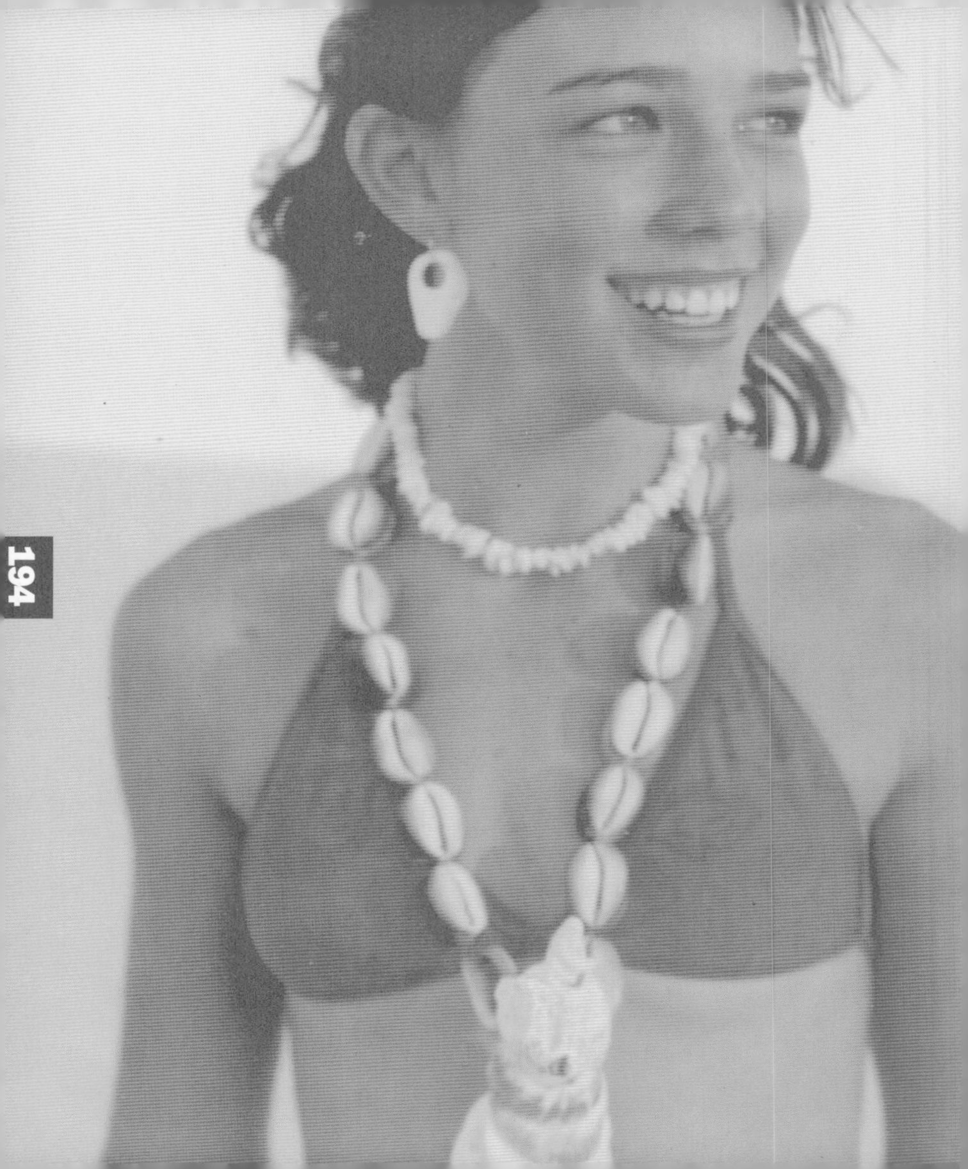

What is your aura saying?

Your thoughts are energy forms that have an impact.
BY THINKING POSITIVE THOUGHTS YOU CAN CHANGE THE
ENERGY YOU PROJECT. ENERGY = AURA.

1. You can always change your mind
2. You can face and eliminate your fears
3. Whatever you expect to happen is what will happen

WELCOME TO YOUR SPIRITUAL REALITY

198

MEDITATE AND RAISE YOUR LEVELS OF CONSCIOUSNESS The Meditation Guide that
simple and highly effective form of meditation you can try at any moment: Sit quietly with
answer come in its own good time. You are requesting help from the Universe! Asking your

199

follows this chapter gives a detailed method of how to meditate, but there is another

your hands folded and eyes closed, and ask: 'What do I need to know right now?' Let the

(higher) connection to the source of all intelligence for the answer is powerful. Try it!

I AM DESERVING

I AM LOVABLE

I AM LOVED

I AM BEAUTIFUL

I AM SUCCESSFUL IN MY
RELATIONSHIPS

I HAVE WHAT I NEED
WITHIN ME

I AM WORTHY

I AM WHOLE AND
COMPLETE

I AM PEACEFUL

I AM BLESSED

I HAVE THE COURAGE TO
MAKE CHANGES

I AM LEARNING WHAT I
NEED FOR MY HIGHEST
GOOD

ETC.

POSITIVE VIBRATIONS ... AFFIRMATIONS

As discussed in the MIND chapter, your outlook can be changed simply by replacing a thought you may have transformed over time into a belief. Changing beliefs can be achieved by turning negative thinking into positive. Affirm that you are deserving and you will be in receiving mode. Wherever you have a belief that's negative, write down its opposite and repeat it. The trick to affirmations is to write them — and then say them — in the present tense. You say them as if they are already a part of your present reality and then you just wait for reality to play catch-up! Try doing it on a daily basis after (or even during) meditation and see what comes. You may be surprised by what you're holding onto.

YOUR THOUGHTS ARE ENERGY: MENTAL = ACTUAL

Taking charge is critical when you're in spiritual recovery.

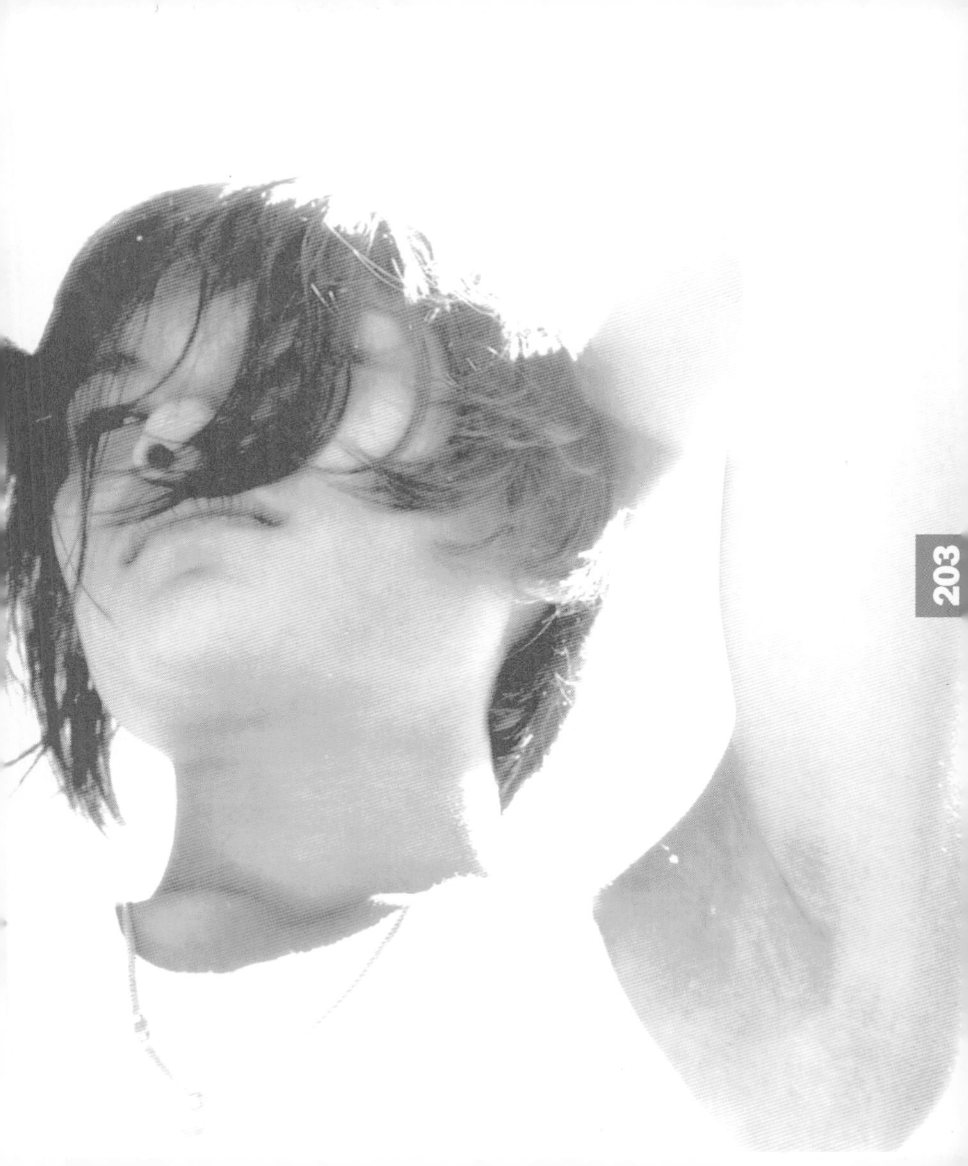

Creative visualization — can you see the future?

As I've said before, life is pictures. Can you see images
of what you imagine your life to be? What does your
spirit want? Who or what inspires you? What makes your
heart sing? The answers to these questions are clues as
to whether you're on the right path. If you honestly don't
know the answers then it's time to find out. Experiment
while you're in this new phase. Explore different options.
Have different experiences. Be ready to experiment with
new activities or people. While you're doing so, draw your
life as you ultimately wish to see it. Check all areas! But —
and this is crucial — don't hold on to or be attached to
the outcome. Ask for it, put it out there but be prepared to
revise any desired goal if ever your spirit feels you must.

It's your reunion...

And if you do decide to get back together with someone, it should be because you've really worked out issues and you are (having decided to be with them again) starting fresh — as far as this is possible. Ensure that you are getting back together for the right reasons and agree to treat it like a new relationship. Set a few ground rules. Let the past be what it is: in the past. You have already forgiven the other person (if you've been doing your homework that is!). Bring your new self to the table. Insist that they do too. Be as open, honest and clear as you can. Enjoy the brand new opportunity you have before you. You have much more self-knowledge and that will only make you stronger, better, more confident, more spiritually aware. It really is ALL good!

Um, have we met before? Congratulations
brilliantly from the ashes of what looked like
only possibility. You are pure potential. Don't

PHOENIX RISING

it's a brand new you! You've emerged a disaster, and in your magnificence you see be afraid. Go forth and be compelling — you are! The whole world is waiting for you…

The bigger picture, for your consideration ... Be vigilant and do the right thing for yourself then a real soulmate (one who's still out there) will be able to recognize you!

at every step on the journey. Think of it this way: when you honor and are true to yourself,

THE
30-DAY
POST-
BREAKUP
DAILY
JOURNAL

THE 30-DAY POST-BREAKUP DAILY JOURNAL

This is a practical section that needs your input to be truly effective. Whether you have come upon this book two months after a breakup or two minutes, the following journal can be a great way to do some personal work and track your own progress. It is also a way to check-in to YOUR needs, keeping the focus solely on you and what you need to get through your day/week/month.

The categories are there as a basic guide. For instance, Inspiration may be a film you saw, book you read, magazine article, a beautiful garden, a view ... anything that gave you pleasure or joy. For the Realization section, you could write down what it was that you got from the inspiration. For example, if you saw a beautiful flower, you may have the realization that nature is the ultimate teacher. Likewise, the Lessons Learned space may be anything you thought of during the day that you wish to record — for instance, giving a complement to a stranger and then having someone give you one later that day or just noticing something as you drive past it. There may be days when you can't fill every category, and that's perfectly fine too — it's up to you and how you want to work the journal.

The journal is designed to get you past the wallowing/deep grief stage, however, the length of this will depend on your personal circumstances. After, say, six months, if you are still making no progress (i.e. you are still depressed, obsessing or exhibiting other symptoms of grief) then it may be time to bring in the heavy artillery — Mom, Dad, or your family doctor. You can't muck around with depression. You need to get it treated. Seriously. It's an illness and these days there is much that can be done to help you through it. The same goes for anyone you know who you think hasn't got past a relationship breakdown after a decent amount of time. Be a true friend and talk to them gently about enlisting some outside assistance.

Remember: right now it's all about you and your recovery. The Post-Breakup Daily Journal will hopefully help you maintain your (positive) lifestyle management strategies and clue you in to what may need your attention. Photocopy the template on the following pages or use the format in your own diary and get started.

Here's to all the happiness that's coming your way!

DATE: _____

MIND: _____

DAILY MEDITATION: _____MINUTES

POSITIVE THOUGHTS: _____

_____

_____

_____

AFFIRMATIONS:_____

_____

_____

NEGATIVE THOUGHTS: _____

_____

REPLACED WITH: _____

_____

OVERALL MOOD _____(out of 10)

BODY:_____

DAILY FOOD PLAN:_____

Breakfast _____

Lunch_____

Dinner _____

Snacks _____

VITAMIN SUPPLEMENTS:

List: _____

_____

WATER INTAKE: _____Liters

214

PHYSICAL ACTIVITY:_____
_____

REST/SLEEP (LAST NIGHT) _____

SPIRIT:_____

INSPIRATION: _____
_____
_____

REALIZATION: _____

MANTRA:_____
_____

MEDITATION:_____(minutes)

READING:_____(pages/chapters) in _____ (time)

LESSONS LEARNED (if any): _____
_____
_____
_____
_____

GENERAL VIBE (description of day):_____
_____
_____
_____
_____
_____

DAY RATING:_____(out of ten)

MEDITATION: YOUR QUICK STEP-BY-STEP GUIDE

As mentioned in the MIND Chapter, to make an effective request of the Universe, your mind needs to be static-free — that is, free from too many overlapping and conflicting thoughts. When you desire a clear response, just as you do in any situation, you have to make a clear request. Thoughts are energy and so if you are sending out a thought amidst a whole bunch of other jumbled up thoughts, it has a greater chance of getting lost in the maelstrom. If you find that when you have asked your question you don't get some sort of clarity, it's likely that you were in the static zone! Meditation is a heightened form of concentration. It can be a very calming and powerful method of rewiring yourself for a positive outlook and enhancing your focus on any goal.

You have to be in the right mind for things to come in at the right time!

Here's a brief run-down on one meditation technique to help you become clear and focused ... and static-free! There are many forms of meditation, however, and (as with anything) the technique you choose is about what works best for you. You may need to experiment and/or research other methods if after a reasonable number of attempts this method doesn't seem to be effective for you. This is the breath-observation method, and it will get you into the zone if you practice it. Choose a time when you won't be disturbed by anyone. This is your precious time.

Preparation:

First, take off your watch or set an alarm clock for a few minutes' time. Get comfortable by either sitting on your bed with your feet on the floor or sitting on the floor with your legs crossed and your spine against the wall for support. You can even sit on a chair or, if you prefer, lie on the floor. Whatever feels right for you.

Step 1. Breathe in through your nose with your mouth closed.

Step 2. Leave your eyes either half-open and focused on one point in the room or, if you prefer, close them fully.

Step 3. Continue to breathe through your nose until you feel the breath go all the way to your stomach, and then breathe out the same way so you can feel a kind of 'loop' pattern in your breathing.

Step 4. Don't follow any train of thought (this can be hard but you have to try) and if any thoughts arise, let them fall away as you return your focus to your breath.

Step 5. The thoughts will continue to come — the trick is to learn to ignore them. They have no place for you right now because they are only serving to distract you from your mission of being peacefully static-free! If you find you have too many thoughts, practice running an affirmation over and over in your mind. For example: 'I love my life. I am happy and contented. All is well in my world.' You can change the meditation to suit your needs or your mood.

Step 6. Be still, don't fidget and try to control any excess body movement. Focus.

Step 7. Do this for as long as you can. You can start with a few minutes and work up to longer periods. Do it first thing in the morning when you're fresh, and then again in the evening before you go to sleep.

It may seem like hard work, but the more you meditate the greater the results.

THE CHAKRA SYSTEM: A QUICK OVERVIEW

Traditionally, there are said to be seven chakras. Each chakra is associated with a particular region of the body with its own purpose and each is a source for healing therapy. Here's the quick list:

Crown Chakra (top of your head in the center)

Third Eye Chakra (between your eyebrows)

Throat Chakra (center-front of your neck region)

Heart Chakra (center of your chest)

Solar Plexus or Power Chakra (located under your rib cage)

Lower Abdomen or Sacral Chakra, aka the Sex Chakra (just below your navel)

Base Chakra (located directly underneath the base of your pelvis).

Are your chakras in balance or out of whack?

When any of the chakras are out of balance, healing is required. You can tell when your chakras are 'in balance' because everything just feels good — you feel on track and full of purpose and you have a clear view of your unique role in life. When your chakras are balanced, basically you are in tune with the universal flow or vibe — you can feel it and somehow you just know that you are!

If you're out of whack, re-balancing the chakras restores vitality and unity not only to their combined functioning, but to your whole body. Mantras (repeated affirmations or prayers while you meditate) and tones (for example the word OM, hummed at a certain level) re-balance each chakra. Massage is another way of restoring balance. Ultimately, having and maintaining balanced chakras is essential for your individual soul to be united with the collective or universal soul.

Think of it this way: if you put one vertebra in your back out, it affects your whole back. The chakras function in exactly the same way, where each contributes to and affects the whole system. Below is a breakdown of each of the chakras' properties and qualities.

First chakra: base (root) chakra

Where do I find it? Base of the spine, under the pelvis.

What's it all about? Here the individual being is linked with the world in physical form. This is the basis for self-expression and ambition, tempered by the desire to evolve, protect self and survive. The base chakra is at the foundation of existence upon which the personality is built, in ultimate connection to the Divine Source.

What's my mantra? I am understood and express myself as a physical being which is constantly evolving.

Related body parts: Adrenal glands, lymph system, colon and intestines, bones, teeth, nails, legs, arms.

Associated color: Red.

In balance? You recognize the material world is the ground level of existence but you maintain a clear view to the spiritual. In this state you are deeply connected to nature and yet you trust implicitly in the universal laws. Stability is sought and self-reliance and independence are the end-goal. You have appropriate personal boundaries in place and you respect the boundaries of others.

Out of whack? The material world is overwhelmingly your focus and matters of spiritual concern are disregarded and ignored. The pursuit of personal material gain is your sole purpose and your ego rules your basic survival instinct, preventing your heart from alerting you to universal energies. Insecurity, greed and stress are your primary life experience. You have an inability to let go and to 'flow and let flow'. Your personal boundaries are weak and you crash in on the boundaries of others without consideration. Phew!

Second chakra: lower abdomen (sex) chakra

Where do I find it? Lower abdomen up to the navel area.

What's it all about? This chakra is the center of creativity, relationships and sexuality. Here the 'male' and 'female' energies are harmoniously blended and balanced to create relationships, which serve the intentions of the Divine Source.

What's my mantra? I express and give birth to my self by using the sex drive to channel creativity and beauty.

Related body parts: Genitals, reproductive organs, spleen, bladder, kidneys.

Associated color: Orange.

In balance? You give and receive in equal measure without difficulty. You're a star! You surrender to the process of sharing and your relationships are harmonious and deeply connected. Your openness of heart, body and mind ensure that joy is your life experience. Your sexuality is expressed with unity and spirituality.

Out of whack? You have an inability to give or receive and find it hard to surrender to universal energies. You may be locked into the purely physical or functional expression of sexuality. You try to control situations and emotions in relationships, which leads to repression of needs and (healthy) expression. Jealousy and mistrust are symptoms of a closed heart, mind and body.

Third chakra: solar plexus (power) chakra

Where do I find it? The solar plexus (under the rib cage) including the region above the navel.

What's it all about? This chakra rules the impulses and is the center of desire. Your personality is integrated here with your impulses, your free will, wishes and the expression of personal power. That's why it's often referred to as the power chakra!

What's my mantra? I am a being who expresses my personality through my free will and in accordance with my desires.

Related body parts: Adrenal glands, pancreas, nervous system, abdomen, lower back, stomach, liver, spleen, digestive system, gall bladder.

Associated color: Yellow.

In balance? Your emotions are vital and free-flowing! You have an overriding sense of tranquility and you generally exist in a state of calmness. Free will and personal power are each exercised intuitively and spontaneously without fear. Basically, you are pretty cool.

Out of whack? Well, it goes like this: emotional blockages are common and panic is the overwhelming feeling. You are incapable of trusting in the process or 'going with the flow' and you place too much emphasis on getting your own way, ignoring the better solution for the greater good. Anger, fear and hatred are common responses. Scary.

Fourth chakra: heart chakra

Where do I find it? Center of chest, heart region.

What's it all about? Your heart is the heart of the chakra system! It mediates between the top three and the lower three chakras. It is the great processor through which all emotion, compassion and intuition is channeled. It's doing a lot of work if you're in sync! Healing and emotions are generated and balanced by free-flowing love.

What's my mantra? I love myself and this love is then expressed to the whole, which is equally loved.

Related body parts: Heart, circulatory or arterial system, rib cage, upper back, arms, lungs, hands.

Associated color: Green.

In balance? Unconditional love is freely offered and your connection to the spiritual and physical (the natural environment) world reflects your state of passion, bliss and joy. You tend to see and accept the positive aspects of all events in life. To you, no matter what: it's ALL good!

Out of whack? Problems with the heart recur. Anger and fear rule your reactions and impulses. Freedom from worry is all but impossible. You may not have the ability to be compassionate and selfishness becomes habitual. Love given is conditional and transactional. Ka-ching!

Fifth chakra: throat chakra

Where do I find it? The throat area, underneath the chin and above the inner collarbone.

What's it all about? This chakra relates to how you communicate your emotions. It also assists you in the transition towards inward reflection. It's the base for all aspects of sound on the physical and vibrational (or metaphysical) planes. It's your voice, your laughter, how you cry, shout or whisper. It's your self as you truly express it!

What's my mantra? I am a being who is freely able to communicate my essence to the Universe.

Related body parts: Throat, thyroid, vocal cords, lungs, neck.

Associated colors: Cyan, turquoise, light blue.

In balance? Harmonious, powerful and clear communication of the truth. You face and express reality easily and readily without fear or favor. It's ON! You are creatively tuned into the divine, and you are powerful as a communicator even when you are silent. You trust and act upon your intuition above all and without hesitation.

Out of whack? Your knowledge is not communicated well or wisely. Um, er, things are misinterpreted or misunderstood and your explanations are clouded or distorted perceptions of the truth. Hmmm ... Ignorance or a lack of discernment can be a symptom of imbalance in this chakra as well as mild to chronic depression. You have a fear of speaking your truth. Oops.

Sixth chakra: third eye chakra

Where do I find it? Center of your forehead between the eyes/brows.

What's it all about? You perceive yourself as actually 'being'. Your psychic qualities (including your sixth sense!) are activated and your awareness brings you a sense of the cosmic. Concentration and focus lead to the growth of your intuition — (and it's not) your basic instinct! You understand the spiritual connection that reflects truly who you are. This chakra is described as being the gateway for spiritual understanding. It's deep!

What's my mantra? I am a 'knowing' being for whom awareness is all.

Related body parts: Pituitary gland, left eye, sinus, nose, ears.

Associated colors: Indigo, deep marine blue.

In balance? Your psychic, clairvoyant and intuitive side is very active! Vivid dreams are common when your third eye chakra is in balance. Great wisdom and creative solutions are easy to attain (well, they seem easy anyway!). The signs on your spiritual path become easier to read as your awareness level increases.

Out of whack? You only think about the material things in life — spiritual matters don't concern you. It's all about you and your needs. Your intellect dominates your activities and yet concentration is difficult. The conscious mind is often overwhelmed with too many fearful, negative and conflicting thoughts. Spooky stuff!

Seventh chakra: crown chakra

Where do you find it? At the top of your head, in the center.

What's it all about? This chakra is where you (as a beautiful and unique individual!) and the Universe actually connect. The crown chakra represents the culmination of the other six chakras, for here the complete physical, mental and spiritual human is connected with its higher self and the source: pure consciousness.

What's my mantra? I am a pure being with no limitations.

Related body parts: Central nervous system, pineal gland, right eye, brain, cerebellum, skull.

Associated colors: Violet, white, gold.

In balance? You see yourself as being connected to the Divine Source and as a unique individual who is part of the whole. Your focus is on the greater good and 'consciousness', not just on what your own needs are. You are a giver in the fullest sense and you do it not for personal gain, but because you love to and it brings joy to all concerned.

Out of whack? Oh dear! Lets see now ... egocentricity, recurring fears, worries, a sense of confusion, depression, lack of inspiration and/or a general sense of dissatisfaction with life. Hmmm. It's quite a list!

IT'S ALL ABOUT ENERGY!

So, from the above list, you should be able to see (and feel) where you're at. Figuring out the energy levels of each of your chakras may not be easy at first but once you become really familiar with the properties and classic symptoms of each, you'll soon be able to do it without checking. Which is the aim of the whole exercise. Basically, the more you can tune in to yourself, in order to self-diagnose and heal, the sooner you'll be able to cope and deal with whatever gets thrown your way!